THE STORY OF

Miss Saigon

Edward Behr

and

Mark Steyn

ARCADE PUBLISHING · NEW YORK

LITTLE, BROWN AND COMPANY

other books by Edward Behr

THE ALGERIAN PROBLEM
THE THIRTY-SIXTH WAY (with Sidney Liu)
"ANYONE HERE BEEN RAPED AND SPEAKS ENGLISH?"
GETTING EVEN
THE LAST EMPEROR
HIROHITO: BEHIND THE MYTH
LES MISÉRABLES: HISTORY IN THE MAKING
KISS THE HAND YOU CANNOT BITE: THE RISE AND FALL
OF THE CEAUSESCUS

FIRST U.S. EDITION

Miss Saigon lyrics © 1987, 1988, 1989, and 1990 by
Alain Boublil Music Ltd., New York
Rights of dramatic performance for all countries of the world administered
by Cameron Mackintosh Ltd., 1 Bedford Square, London WC1B 3RA
Miss Saigon logo and artwork design © Cameron Mackintosh Ltd.
Miss Saigon graphics designed by Dewynters PLC, London
Copyright for the photographs in this book is held by Michael Le Poer Trench,
unless otherwise specified in the Picture Credits.
Lyrics from *South Pacific* © 1949 by Williamson Music International, USA,
reproduced by permission of EMI Music Publishing Ltd., London

ISBN 1-55970-124-2
Library of Congress Catalog Card Number 90-55916
Library of Congress Cataloging-in-Publication information is available.

Published in the United States by Arcade Publishing, Inc., New York,
a Little, Brown company

10 9 8 7 6 5 4 3 2 1

PRINTED IN THE UNITED STATES OF AMERICA

Contents

(Chapters 1, 3, 7, 9, 10, 12, 14 and 17 are by Edward Behr;
chapters 2, 4, 5, 6, 8, 11, 13, 15 and 16 are by Mark Steyn)

Acknowledgments

We would like to thank all those in London, New York, Los Angeles, Honolulu and Manila who helped to make this book possible:

Cameron Mackintosh, Alain Boublil, Claude-Michel Schönberg, Richard Maltby Jnr, Nicholas Hytner and Jonathan Pryce all gave us vast amounts of their time. So did Bob Avian, William D. Brohn, David Caddick, Herbert Kretzmer, John Napier, David Hersey, Andreane Neofitou, Charlotte Bird, Nguyen and Leon Bartlett, and Vincent Liff of Johnson-Liff Casting Associates.

We would especially like to thank Richard Jay-Alexander, Mitch Lemsky and Cherrie Sciro of Cameron Mackintosh Inc., as well as Alan Wasser, all in New York; and in London, Robert Dewynter, Russ Eglin, Moni Haworth, Anthony Pye-Geary and Peter Thompson.

Many thanks too, to Tommy Aguilar in Honolulu, Zeanida Amador and Baby Barredo of the Philippines Repertory Theatre, 'Dong' Allegre and the staff of the Philippines Cultural Centre in Manila, and, of course, the members of the *Miss Saigon* cast, in particular the three London Kims – Lea Salonga, Monique Wilson and Jenine Desiderio.

Lastly, a very special thank you to Tee Hesketh, whose efficiency, infinite patience and encyclopaedic memory never failed to amaze us.

Picture Credits

A Note on the Bui Doi

We can't forget, must not forget
That they are all our children too.
'Bui Doi', Miss Saigon

It was a photograph of a grieving Vietnamese woman parting with her Amerasian child that inspired the story of *Miss Saigon*. The child in the photograph is one of thousands in the same position, possibly the most helpless, pathetic victims of the Vietnam War.

The *bui doi*, or 'dust of life' as the Vietnamese call them, are, for the most part, the offspring of brief liaisons between bar-girls and American GIs. A tragic legacy of the 'second' Vietnam War, these Amerasian children began life as pariahs, their mixed parentage stamped on their faces: some were freckled and fair-haired – almost indistinguishable from American children; others were dark-haired and dark-skinned, or Vietnamese-looking but for their blue or grey-green eyes. Rejected by neighbours, by other children, and often by family, and unable to enrol in schools, they lived on the streets, exploited and subjected to constant cruelty and humiliation.

Although with the inception of the US State Department's 'Orderly Departure Programme' in 1964, the status of the *bui doi* improved – 33,419 *bui doi* and their families have left Asia, and another 15,000 are expected to leave in 1991 – only 1 per cent of those that have reached the US are said to have found their real fathers. It is likely that the programme will continue for several years, for it is only now that many of the 'dust of life' are daring to come forward and claim their inheritance.

1 *The Saigon of* Miss Saigon

I never knew Saigon in the old days, which were, of course, the days of the French. By the time I arrived, in 1967, the acacia trees lining the once elegant avenues were slowly dying from the effects of diesel fumes and pollution. The French provincial look had wilted; there were landmarks still, like the nineteenth-century Grall hospital, the Opera building (now the National Assembly), and a few unmistakably French *lycées*, but there was a profusion of new, yet already dilapidated office buildings and jerry-built high-rise apartment blocks in hideous pastel colours. Though some traces of 'la mission civilisatrice Française' remained, the current presence was overwhelmingly American. No longer, however, were they Graham Greene's 'Quiet Americans'.

When I first saw it, Saigon was a thoroughly American garrison town. Endless military convoys roared through the streets, belching black smoke. The remains of the French-type paving-stones were being replaced by asphalt; US military policemen, smart as new toys, patrolled the streets; many of the expatriates were civilians, the inevitable hard-faced men (mainly in the construction industry, but also selling everything from computers to pharmaceuticals) making small fortunes out of the war. There were American doctors, dentists, teachers, sociologists and economists, some of them wildly enthusiastic about Vietnam's war-fuelled 'economic miracle', and large numbers of markedly less enthusiastic correspondents. Kerbside stores sold goods stolen or traded from the 'PX' stores – Johnnie Walker Red Label whisky and Old Spice predominating – and there were even minor items of military equipment like belts, embroidered slogans ('I am the meanest son-of-a-bitch in the valley') and the inevitable 'C' rations, as well as buttons and badges that could have originated in Times Square. So prevalent was the black market in almost everything, that newly arrived correspondents were told where the best covered market was to buy US Army uniforms – essential garb for accompanying units on operations, and less trouble to obtain there than from an official army base clothing outlet. There were even rumours that weapons of all kinds from anti-personnel grenades to AK 47s, were obtainable if you had the right contacts. Tough-looking Vietnamese women squatted at street-corners with catalogues of cameras and hi-fi equipment which could be ordered for later delivery, and were, in fact, stolen at source from 'PX' warehouses.

Nowhere was the American presence more visible than in the 'girlie bars' outnumbering the old, fast-vanishing French-style

9

cafés by at least a hundred to one. Here, even in the daytime, a few girls lingered, waiting for the occasional visitor. Just around the corner from the Hotel Continental (where I lived, on and off, and where *Newsweek* was eventually, after the 'Tet 1968' offensive, to move its offices), there was an unusually discreet bar. It was slightly off the beaten track, never full, open for some reason in the daytime more often than in the evenings. I remember the same US Air Force officer, invariably drunk, propping up the bar there most afternoons, and often wondered what it was that attracted him to the place, and how he was able to spend so much time there.

The sounds coming out of the bars were the sounds of the Sixties, hard rock, Nancy Sinatra singing 'These Boots Were Made for Walking', the Rolling Stones, Jimi Hendrix, Janis Joplin. In the evenings, the neon-lit bars were crowded, and most of the customers were GIs. Many of them were Saigon residents: for R & R, the week-long 'Rest & Recreation' all GIs claimed, half-way through their one-year term in Vietnam, the US Army would fly them, at American taxpayers' expense, as far afield as Sydney, Australia.

Most GIs, understandably, had one obsession – to get out of Vietnam for that blessed week. Many preferred the infinitely more luxurious fleshpots of Patpong Road to those of Saigon or Cholon. So the faithful patrons were often 'locals', what in French World War I jargon would have been called *les embusqués*, the shirkers, who, through either influence or good fortune, had found comfortable, if temporary, non-combat assignments in the capital. The real 'fighting men', stuck in the base camps and bunkers that littered the countryside and jungles had fewer opportunities to come to the 'ville', as they called it.

The GIs who returned to the bars, night after night, month after month, were in search of more than just female company; these were the only places where they could, for an hour or two, get away from their army environment and imagine they were back home, sipping ice-cold beer while listening to familiar music. There were of course plenty of establishments like the one near Tan Son Nhut airport, the Artistic Hand Massage Parlour, as well as discreet 'places of assignation' where the girls wore white coats like nurses, but the self-respecting bars in Tu Do street were strictly meeting-places.

I close my eyes, hear the music and catch a whiff of strongly-scented talcum powder. In my mind's eye, I can still see them: their shiny plastic handbags were lined up at one end of the bar; they chattered happily among themselves; a few wore *ao dais* – traditional Vietnamese dress – but most were in miniskirts, or white, frilly blouses and well-cut jeans. Their attire, though discreetly hinting at sexual availability, never, as in Bangkok and especially Vientiane (Laos), bordered on semi-nudity – the Saigon police saw to that. In Vietnam form had always been as important as substance, and something of the puritanism of Madame Nhu, Ngo Dinh Diem's sister-in-law and the 'iron lady' of the Fifties and early Sixties, remained.

Many of the girls had lacquered hair-dos. Some were outrageously made up, or had spent vast sums on plastic surgery to become 'roundeyes', like Madame Ky, the former air-hostess wife of Marshal Ky, one-time Air Force commander and the regime's Number Two at the time. A few were on the squat side, peasant girls in their teens with puppy fat, pouting lips and a vacant, heart-rending innocence. But most had an exotic, natural beauty, even if their lipstick was often bright purple with matching nail varnish and stiletto shoes. Their overall look was sometimes a grotesque parody of Sixties' fashions, culled from dog-eared issues of *Elle*, but they had innate grace and golden skins that made you long to stroke their bare arms.

Their English was rudimentary, but they quickly picked up the GI slang that Michael Herr was later to reproduce so unerringly in *Dispatches*. They were not very efficient hustlers, though their *rasion d'être* was to get GIs to buy them drink after drink. 'You buy me Saigon tea?' (coloured water that looked like whisky and was priced as such) was the preliminary gambit, but if one made an excuse to remain on one's own they didn't seem to mind. The expense of the 'Saigon tea' in the more respectable bars was in any case minimal – at least for a GI with little else on which to spend his money – and the beer only fractionally more expensive than in a Paris-style café.

If you bought a bar-girl a drink, you exchanged names, and this created a bond that was not entirely artificial, for she rarely forgot yours, and if the one you had met the first time was not there you could say: 'Thank you, no, I'm waiting for Gigi,' and this conduct was approved. Of course it often happened that there might be two GIs waiting for the same girl's attentions, but this rarely led to conflict. Both men seemed quite happy, at opposite ends of the bar, to spend a few minutes with the girl they had come to see, and then wait before their drink for her to go from one to another. The semi-darkness of the bars facilitated this vaudevillesque *va-et-vient*.

A discreet voyeur, I admired the girls' dexterity, circulating like fashionable hostesses at embassy receptions. Noticing each others' predicament, they would help their friends out, attracting the attention of the rival so he would not notice 'his' girl and another man kissing. The GIs and bar-girls held hands a lot, and the necking and heavy petting that went on reminded me of the

Fifties as I had vicariously experienced them in American movies.

To an onlooker, it was strangely, unexpectedly, innocent. Of course, by curfew time (11 pm), many couples had left together, but this was by no means always the case. Many of the girls never went home with American soldiers. They had 'permanent arrangements' with a taxi-driver, or a brother, fiancé or husband with a motor-scooter of his own, and it was always a tragi-comic experience to watch some of the GIs left high and dry, their 'Saigon tea' companions snatching up their handbags and leaving suddenly on the stroke of eleven. On Tu Do street, you could set your watch by the roar of scooters and of the tiny, noisy blue-and-yellow Renault taxis. The curfew meant that if a girl went home with her GI to his lodgings or 'hooches' as they were called, they spent the night together.

At the Continental, the rules were less strict than at the Caravelle, where bar-girls were off limits (though in-house prostitutes, far less attractive and far more expensive, openly solicited, and with the management's blessing). The girl simply handed over her ID card to the concierge, who leered at you, and doubtless reported you, later, to the secret police.

It would be hypocritical to pretend that I stumbled on these details through hearsay. These bars fascinated me, and sometimes, though not often, I did not return to my room alone. I remember talking once late into the night, and my companion explaining how she had been a secretary, but this was easier, and better paid. 'We are so poor,' she said. 'You can't imagine how poor my family is.' She told me about her boyfriend, a GI who had left Vietnam the previous year. He had written at first, she said, then the letters had stopped. She eventually showed me one of the early letters. The stilted, banal expressions of love saddened me. I later discovered that it was when she got round to telling him that she was pregnant that the letters ceased. For a while I became a letter-writing go-between, using language she might credibly have used, while she copied my drafts in the childish handwriting she had learnt in a school that still taught French as a second language. Needless to say, I have no idea what happened to her, or her child. The possibility that both may have ended up in a state 'institution' disturbs me to this day.

A French TV documentary, made several years after the collapse of South Vietnam, showed some of these former bar-girls in 'rehabilitation therapy', repeating, parrot-fashion, clichés about American imperialism. The new Vietnamese authorities used these war victims to denounce their former 'oppressors' in terms that were both laughable and wildly inappropriate. *Of course* the whole bar-girl phenomenon had been a by-product of the awful war, but this had not prevented a form of warmth, or, in many cases,

genuine relationships between the Americans far from home and young Vietnamese women. Things were far more complicated than the cliché-ridden Vietnamese functionaries pretended. As I watched the documentary, another image came to mind: of black GIs and their Vietnamese girlfriends laughing, dancing and flirting in a small bar in Cholon with the innocent *abandon* and unselfconscious enjoyment of young people anywhere. I also remember a bar in Danang, a grave-faced but absurdly young GI breaking the news to one of the girls that one of her boyfriends had just been killed, and the heart-rending sobs that would not stop.

The extreme youth of the GIs in Vietnam has been hammered home in countless books and films about the war. The girls were often even younger: both sides were inexperienced, unprepared for tragedy, full of absurd juvenile buoyancy, and the mercantile aspect of bar-girl sex didn't preclude moments of pure joy.

It is easy, at this distance from events, to become judgmental. The bar-girl phenomenon *was* regrettable, and the girls *were*, in a sense, prostitutes, though even the 'Gigis' among them, on whom the hard-bitten, experienced girl in *Miss Saigon* is modelled, lacked the haggard toughness of their Western counterparts. And, of course, the exploitation, not only by Americans, but by Vietnamese and Chinese entrepreneurs, functioning with the complicity of a predatory police force and military regime, was brutal. There were tales, too, of mothers selling their daughters, of Vietnamese 'cowboys' seducing innocent girls and becoming their pimps. Outside Saigon, there were grimmer places, like the notorious garages where US Army truck drivers could get their vehicles hosed down by Vietnamese soldiers while enjoying a 'short time' upstairs with their girls. But the sex scene, in comparison with what it had been under French rule (with the huge brothel complex, 'Le Grand Monde') was less organised, and probably more innocent. The French had done things differently. Their colonial officials had picked out barely nubile orphans from religious institutions for domestic service and sexual enslavement, sometimes with the tacit connivance of the nuns themselves. 'Le Grand Monde' apart, there had been officially run army brothels – Bordels Militaires de Campagne (BMCs) – in every large barracks, and some in the field – there was even one at the siege of Dien Bien Phu. In the final analysis, which form of exploitation was more humane?

Miss Saigon's 'Engineer', who does his best to exploit Kim and her child while attempting to feather his own nest, was certainly an archetypal character. In real life as in the theatre, however, he too was vulnerable. Even in the time of the French, Vietnam was full of small-time hustlers who never quite made it – Corsicans, Vietnamese, and, in the twilight of the war, even Americans. It's fair to say that, for all the corruption and theft on a large scale during the American war years, the fortunes made by these individual predators were probably less huge than those resulting from the French Indochina war's scam, the 'trafic des piastres'. This involved the endless recycling of money to take advantage of the overvalued Indochinese piastre, with banks, corporations and political parties all benefiting. During the 'American' war, more people were involved because the war was on a vast scale. Like the 'Engineer', many of them were pathetically modest operators, and for all the prevalence of corruption in official circles, some Vietnamese army officers and government officials retained their integrity: many of the refugees once in high places, fleeing Vietnam after 1975, started life afresh in menial jobs in Europe and the US because they had been too honest to acquire a nest-egg.

With all this in mind, the opening number of *Miss Saigon* is for me far more convincing than almost any bar scene in the sixty-odd films that have been made about the Vietnam War. In particular the Tu Do street scene in *The Deer Hunter* (actually shot in Thailand) was far too frenzied, the sex too overt, the music too loud, the backdrop too luxurious. Even during the closing stages of the war, though bars and massage parlours were tolerated, their owners were cautioned to behave with discretion. In *The Deer Hunter*, a bar-girl go-go dancer takes Christoper Walken back to her tiny apartment and prepares to make love while her baby is awake and crying in the same room. Perhaps more than anything else, this scene reduced the film's credibility in the eyes of Vietnam veterans: they knew no Vietnamese woman would ever have made love to a customer in front of her baby. The innate modesty of Vietnamese women, and the powerful religious impact, both Buddhist and Catholic, left their mark throughout the war: many bar-girls were monogamists at heart, genuinely seeking a relationship where dependency and genuine emotion were as important as financial security. Understandably, they wanted to survive, to experience 'the American dream'.

Another way of escaping from celibacy and loneliness could be found in the two English-language newspapers in Saigon, which carried daily advertisements from firms specialising in negotiating permanent or semi-permanent relationships between expatriate males (Americans preferred) and Vietnamese girls. Legal documents were drawn up, advice given (the US military authorities made it extremely difficult for GIs to marry Vietnamese in Vietnam itself while still serving there) and while many such relationships ended long before the April–May 1975 débâcle, many more survived. Americans who entered into such an arrangement found it expensive, for they quickly discovered that it entailed supporting an entire Asian family, but in practice they were, like *Madame*

Butterfly's Pinkerton, 'free . . . to annul the marriage monthly. America for ever'. And again, like Pinkerton, many Americans – even those who entered into semi-permanent written 'agreements' – were doubtless looking beyond Vietnam 'to the day on which I'll wed in real marriage – a real American wife!'

Most of the heads of these 'agencies' were lawyers, and many were women. The fees were high, on both sides. The lawyers knew, through their own private information network, how much each American client was worth; their understanding of US military pay scales was highly sophisticated and their rapacity legendary. I was witness to this when one of our staff correspondents, François Sully, was killed during the war in a helicopter crash. He had been a Saigon resident ever since the days of the French, and had accumulated more belongings than the average expatriate, including a furnished flat, two cars (one of them permanently parked in Pnom Penh, where it remained until eventually it disappeared), and a substantial piastre bank balance. Since he left behind a bevy of Vietnamese girlfriends, having promised marriage to all of them, the situation was emotionally as well as financially fraught, and the settlement of his estate a complicated, lengthy undertaking. When it was completed, the Vietnamese lawyer's fees came to within a small fraction of his total Vietnamese assets.

In the light of all this, I am perhaps well-placed to answer the question: is the character of *Miss Saigon* believable? At first, its authors were not overly concerned with total, one hundred per cent, historical accuracy. Theirs was a love story, along the lines of *Madame Butterfly* – and whoever, at the time, questioned the authenticity of Butterfly, Pinkerton or Goro? But it was a love story within the framework of a major international tragedy, which happened to be the end of the Vietnam War, so the question of accuracy is relevant.

I believe that not only Kim, but also Chris, are believable characters. In real life, of course, they would have been less articulate. But within the framework of sung-through theatre, in what is an opera of the Nineties rather than a 'musical', Alain Boublil and Claude-Michel Schönberg have invested them with the kind of truth we perceive in major classic operatic roles. How they came into being, and how Cameron Mackintosh, on the basis of a vague, intuitive hunch, took Schönberg and Boublil's unfinished draft and raised the team that turned it into *Miss Saigon* as first seen at London's Drury Lane Theatre on 20 September 1989, is the subject of this book.

A country boy acts as pimp at a brothel set in a paddy field

2 From Butterflies to Bar-girls

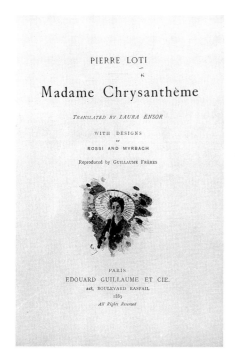

Nippon. The Floating Kingdom. An island empire which for centuries has lived in perfect peace, undisturbed by intruders from across the sea . . .

With John Weidman's opening lines to the 1976 Broadway show *Pacific Overtures*, western *japonisme* came full circle: a musical about America's and Europe's relationship with Japan, but told from a Japanese point of view, taking us back beyond Commodore Perry's 'opening' of the country in 1854 to the complacent serenity of a refined civilisation undisturbed for generations. Within a few decades, all that had changed. For the Western traveller, roaming the world with the blithe confidence which comes from being a citizen of the Great Powers, no destination was as alluring as Japan, not only because of its long isolation from the rest of the world, but also for its location on Eurocentric maps: discounting Australia and other comparatively tame outposts of Empire, Japan was as Far East as you could go. Furthermore, whereas in other far-flung corners of the globe 'native' culture was seen by the Imperial Powers as crude and primitive (all wattle daubs and shrunken heads), Japanese art had an exquisite purity, an almost hypnotic simplicity. To many in the West, *ukiyo-e*, the 'floating world' of the Japanese print, was irresistible.

Within a few years, these influences were reflected in almost every branch of Western art: painting, music, literature, as well as less elevated forms such as interior design. Indeed, Manet's portrait of Zola surrounded by wood-block prints could stand for the almost total infiltration of *japonaiserie* into European culture.

One topic, though, dominated all else – a potent intensification of popular art's favourite theme, 'boy meets girl', which found its most enduring legend in *Madame Chrysanthemum*, an autobiographical novel by Pierre Loti, who'd served with the French Navy in the Far East. Told in diary entries, the story has a minimal plot, but its effectiveness at imparting mood and atmosphere is not to be despised. Pierre, a naval officer stationed at Nagasaki in 1885, eases his stay by entering into a temporary 'marriage' with a geisha girl, a routine arrangement of the time which suited both the foreigners and their 'wives'. In Loti's story, the hero (himself) is a charming witty sophisticate, while the heroine Ki-Hou-San (Chrysanthemum) is practical and unsentimental. Any sense of regret Pierre might have felt at their parting vanishes when he finds her counting the coins he has given her 'with the competence and dexterity of an old moneylender', and waiting for her next 'husband'.

André Messager's operatic version of *Madame Chrysanthemum* first produced in 1893, maintained the popularity of Loti's story until well into this century. In its way, it is not unrealistic: Chrysanthemum was typical of geishas in Nagasaki and the other treaty ports – girls from the countryside whose families sold them into this lucrative business to boost their meagre income. But a hardheaded operator like Ki-Hou-San is not really the stuff of musical theatre heroines. Loti's story was to undergo extensive reconstruction before it finally emerged in its most successful version.

In 1898, the American *Century Magazine* published another story about a Japanese 'marriage' at Nagasaki, this time called *Madame Butterfly*. Its author, John Luther Long, had never visited Japan, but his sister, Mrs Irwin Corell, the wife of a Christian missionary, knew Nagasaki well and, although Long follows Loti's novel extremely closely, it's probable that his version too was prompted by a true story told to him by his sister. According to some experts, the real-life Butterfly was Tsuru Yanamura, whose son was removed to Nagasaki by his father, a British merchant, and educated by Long's nephew. The geisha attempted suicide, but was discovered in time and eventually died peacefully in Tokyo in 1899.

Whatever its origins, Long's story is an almost exact inversion of Loti's. Instead of the likeable French naval captain, there is Lieutenant Pinkerton, cruel, thoughtless, selfish: 'There's no danger of you losing your head to anyone,' a friend tells him. Meeting his new Japanese in-laws, he tells one of them, 'You look exactly like a lacquered tragedy mask I have hanging over my desk.' His American wife Adelaide (Kate in the stage versions) proves to be equally insensitive. At the consulate, she runs into Butterfly without knowing who she is: 'How very charming – how *lovely* – you are dear!' gushes Mrs Pinkerton patronisingly. 'Will you kiss me, you pretty – *plaything*.' It is not only Western *men* who regard Oriental women as amusing toys.

Long's story is no masterpiece, but it has some deft touches, like Cio-Cio-San's lullaby for her (and Pinkerton's) baby:

> Rog-a-by, bebby, off in Japan,
> You jus' a picture off of a fan.

She has, of course, learnt this jingle from Pinkerton who used to sing it to her. When she realises that her beloved Lieutenant has an American consort 'more beautiful than the Sun-Goddess', she comes to her decision, reaches for her father's sword and reads the inscription:

> To die with Honour,
> When one can no longer live with Honour.

. . . She placed the point of the weapon at that nearly nerveless spot in the neck known to every Japanese, and began to press it slowly inward. She could not help a little gasp at the first incision. But presently she could feel the blood finding its way down her neck. It divided on her shoulder, the larger stream going down her bosom. In a moment she could see it making its way daintily between her breasts. It began to congeal there. She pressed on the sword, and a fresh stream swiftly overran the other – redder, she thought. And then suddenly she could no longer see it. She drew the mirror closer. Her hand was heavy, and the mirror seemed far away. She knew that she must hasten. But even as she locked her fingers on the serpent of the guard, something within her cried out piteously. They had taught her how to die, but he had taught her how to live – nay, to make life sweet. Yet that was the reason she must die. Strange reason! She now first knew that it was sad to die. He had come, and substituted himself for everything; he had gone, and left her nothing – nothing but this.

Long's story caused a sensation in the United States, and the author found himself besieged by showfolk wishing to acquire the stage rights, among them two of the American theatre's greatest stars, Julia Marlowe and Maude Adams. In the end, he gave permission to David Belasco, the predominant producer, director and playwright of his day: a compleat showman. In later years, visitors to his office at Broadway's Belasco Theatre had to pass down an endless corridor lined with faithful servants before reaching the inner sanctum, where they would be announced by several prolonged gong-strokes. Inside, in the midst of an elaborate display of Japanese screens bearing the manuscripts of his plays and behind a table strewn with Oriental pottery, sat Belasco himself, white hair tumbling over his forehead and, in the manner of the abbé Liszt, a clerical collar round his neck.

Posterity scoffs at Belasco, the freakish colossus of a theatrical age long gone. Yet many contemporary practitioners could learn from his attention to detail: in rehearsal for *The Darling of the Gods*, he once berated the lighting electrician, 'I don't want a mere moon, I want a *Japanese* moon.' An obsessive 'realist' in his stagings, he insisted, for example, in a scene laid at a Child's restaurant on having fresh coffee brewed and pancakes fried and flipped. If this seems a rather limited approach to theatrical art, it served him well in his adaptation of *Madame Butterfly*. The drama began with a series of illuminated screens, introducing the audience to Japanese

20

rice-fields, cherry-blossomed gardens, fishing boats and a snow-capped volcano in the moonlight. But his finest *coup de théâtre* was the night vigil, in which Butterfly, her child and Suzuki the maid, await the return of Pinkerton. Ring Lardner once wrote a facetious stage direction, 'The curtain is lowered for two weeks to denote the passing of two weeks.' That conflict between the need to convey the passage of time and the audience's boredom threshold has rarely found as finely balanced a solution as Belasco's. As his characters wait and watch, night falls, stars appear, and the lanterns lit to celebrate Pinkerton's return die one by one, leaving the stage in total darkness; then, slowly, dawn breaks, and the birds begin to sing. Twelve hours have passed in fourteen silent minutes which held Belasco's Broadway and West End audiences spellbound. It was this scene which confirmed the showman's pre-eminence as 'the wizard of the stage', and which most impressed Giacomo Puccini when he saw the play at the Duke of York's Theatre in London in 1900.

Miss Evelyn Millard as Madame Butterfly at the Duke of York's Theatre, 1900

Belasco's theatrical powers were at their peak at this time, and his *Butterfly* was a considerable improvement on its predecessors. Few theatregoers were able to staunch their tears as, recalling the Lieutenant's promise to return when 'robins nest again', Cio-Cio-San, breathes her last in Pinkerton's arms: 'Too bad those robins didn' nes' again.' Puccini, although he barely understood the English dialogue, knew a hit property when he saw one, and went backstage to ask Belasco for permission to musicalise *Butterfly*.

In adapting the play, Puccini and his librettists Giacosa and Illica stayed close to their source. The composer was particularly anxious to recreate the night vigil, complete with a dawn chorus from the birds in the trees. On the opera's first night at La Scala on 17 February 1904, the twittering birds greeted the sunrise and unleashed from the audience what Rosina Storchio (playing Butterfly) called a Noah's Ark of barnyard responses. As the birds cheeped and chirped, the audience joined in with cock-a-doodle-doos, donkey brays, loud mooing, before degenerating into undisguised shrieking. Earlier, when a draught from the wings had inflated Storchio's kimono, some wag had jeered, 'Butterfly is pregnant,' and another had answered more viciously, 'Yes – with Toscanini's child!' – a reference to her affair with the distinguished conductor.

The derision was not entirely spontaneous, for a cabal of Puccini's enemies had had it in for him anyway. But no other opera has ever recovered from such a violent opening night fiasco to earn so secure a place in the permanent repertoire. Puccini, Giacosa and Illica withdrew the piece, reworked it (giving Kate Pinkerton's song to Cio-Cio-San, among other things) and emerged with a work which took the Crysanthemum/Butterfly story to its apogee.

21

If not quite a merchandising spin-off on the scale of *Les Misérables* or *Phantom of the Opera*, *Madame Butterfly* started a craze, especially in America, for Japanese kimonos, and Puccini found himself declining endless invitations personally to endorse various brands. In the years since, though, the influence of the work has been mainly musical. Among several songs inspired by the opera is that beautiful standard 'Poor Butterfly', the prolific Raymond Hubbell's only lasting melody. Introduced in *The Big Show*, which opened at the New York Hippodrome in August 1916, it was supposed to be sung by a famous Japanese soprano, Tamaki Miura, for whom John Golden's mawkish lyric had been specifically tailored. She never made it, but the song did.

Other Broadway writers were also attracted to the theme, including the young Oscar Hammerstein II, who attempted in an early work to transfer the cross-cultural romance to other climes: an American soldier is torn between his love for 'Toinette in France and the hometown girl he left behind. *Joan of Arkansas*, as it was rather unwisely called, was not a hit. Hammerstein had to wait thirty years before he was able to rework the *Butterfly* theme in *South Pacific* (1949) and *The King and I* (1951). The former, set in the Pacific during World War II, contains one of Hammerstein's most forthright lyrics, as Lieutenant Cable, in love with a native girl, refuses to accept that racism is man's natural state.

> You've got to be taught to be afraid
> Of people whose eyes are oddly made
> And people whose skin is a diff'rent shade,
> You've got to be carefully taught.
> You've got to be taught
> Before it's too late,
> Before you are six or seven or eight
> To hate all the people your relatives hate . . .

You could argue that, ultimately, Rodgers and Hammerstein duck the question, as Lieutenant Cable conveniently dies in action, before he has to decide whether to take the Polynesian girl back to America with him. And, besides, even well meaning liberals like Hammerstein seem unable to make Oriental women anything other than passive non-characters. In his play *M. Butterfly*, David Henry Hwang turned the myth on its head, showing how a shrewd Oriental could play to advantage a Westerner's need for a passive Butterfly. Based on a true story, it concerns a French diplomat stationed in China who pursues an affair with a beautiful Oriental woman without ever discovering that she was actually male – and a spy. The producer Stuart Ostrow had commissioned Hwang to write a musical, and was rather shocked when he was sent a straight play. 'Oh, shit! I thought. And then I figured I might as well produce it anyway,' he told me. Had he insisted on the story being told musically, the West End might have ended up with two musicals on the Butterfly theme side by side – the Hwang story and *Miss Saigon*. As it was, Hwang and his lead actor, B. D. Wong, were subsequently to cross Cameron Mackintosh's path in a way he could never have foreseen.

If, thanks to Belasco and Puccini, the Butterfly view of Eastern women has become a Western cliché (in everything from high art to commercials for Singapore Airlines), the benign image of Japan has not survived. Nine days after *Madame Butterfly*'s première at La Scala, the Russo-Japanese war began, a conflict which the scholar William Schwartz attributes (in the *Imaginative Interpretation of the Far East in Modern French Literature*), at least in part, to Pierre Loti: 'I believe that the contempt for the Japanese expressed in Loti's books in some measure influenced the Russians to refuse Japan's requests and led to the war of 1904. The Russian Court was open to French influence, and many Russian naval officers of high rank, following Loti's example, had discovered *Madame Chrysanthème*. Like Loti, the Russian Court looked upon Japan with contempt, and chose to believe his stories because Loti shared their prejudices.'

Madame Butterfly, Berlin, 1906

The following year, 1905, thanks to Admiral Togo's destruction of the Tsar's navy, Russia was resoundingly defeated – and, in that humiliation of a European power, modern Japan was born. What price now poor Butterfly? Today, mention of Nagasaki conjures neither Cio-Cio-San's flower garden nor that novelty hit of the Twenties, by Harry Warren and Mort Dixon:

> Back in Nagasaki
> Where the fellers chew tobaccy
> And the women wicky wacky woo . . .

Instead, the name symbolises the lengths to which the Americans, British and French – the nations most seduced by *japonisme* – had to go to vanquish the real Japan. Some time after the atomic bomb was dropped, it was decided to erect a statue of Madame Butterfly in the town – on the estate of Tom Glover, the Scots merchant who introduced whisky to Japan and who, according to some, was the lover of the real-life Butterfly. In its complex intertwining of fiction and fact, this monument represents as well as anything the illusions which have so misled both East and West, and the yawning gulf which still separates the two cultures.

3 *The Origins of* Miss Saigon

At the height of the Vietnam War, and just as the talks in Paris between North Vietnamese and American officials were getting under way, 'May 1968' began. It started as a protest movement at Nanterre, where a puritanical university president had decreed that men's and women's sleeping quarters had to remain rigidly segregated. De Gaulle's ministers' inept handling of it caused it to spread to the Sorbonne, to the Latin Quarter and finally throughout universities and 'lycées' all over France. To everyone's surprise, the French working class, not usually enamoured of student movements, joined in. Workers and students were temporarily united. To some extent their bond was cemented by the impact of the anti-Vietnam war movement in the United States, already prominently highlighted in the French media.

Like millions of other young Frenchmen, Alain Boublil and Claude-Michel Schönberg, who, some twenty years later, would write the words and music for *Miss Saigon*, followed the course of the Vietnam War with interest, but without any insider expertise. 'In 1965, I was twenty-one and a student at "Ecole Supérieure de Commerce" in Nantes, Brittany,' says Schönberg. 'In those days, they ran newsreels in movie-houses, and I remember seeing shots of GIs on patrol and wondering: What on earth are they doing so far from home? In our minds they weren't winning outright because they didn't *want* to win: An A-bomb on Hanoi and it would be all over, for what country could really measure up to the might of the US?'

From 1963–67 Schönberg's abiding interest was not in Vietnam, but in a pop group he had put together called Les Venètes (as the inhabitants of Vannes, his home town, are called), which played nightly gigs in night-clubs all over the region. Schönberg played the piano, arranged bookings, and was the group's acknowledged leader. 'We relied on the group to see us through college,' he says. 'I couldn't have done so without the money we raked in.'

In 1966, a Pathé-Marconi executive and talent scout had spotted Schönberg, and promised him a job as junior artistic director of this large record company. 'I played my last gig on the last day of August, 1967,' says Schönberg, and on 1 September was in Paris, going to work for Pathé-Marconi for the first time.

'We were,' he says, 'extraordinarily ignorant where the world of US musical comedy was concerned. I had heard and loved "West Side Story", but it was a long time before I discovered who Leonard Bernstein was, let alone Stephen Sondheim; I went to see the movie of "My Fair Lady" but couldn't have told you who the composer or the librettist were. I liked my new job very much. I'd spent all my life in the small town of Vannes and here I was shaking hands with people like Frank Aeamo and Dick Rivers!

'Our first understanding of the consequences of the Vietnam War, and its impact on Americans, came with the "Woodstock" concert film,' Schönberg recalls. 'This made us realise, for the first time, that the war was also being fought at home, on the ideological front, and that large numbers of young Americans were passionately anti-war.'

In 1972, the year the US wound down its own operations in Vietnam, handing over more and more responsibility for the war to the South Vietnamese, Alain Boublil went to a première that, quite literally, changed his life: this was *Jesus Christ Superstar* to which he was invited almost by accident after another guest had dropped out. 'Afterwards I wandered the streets of New York all night in a daze,' Boublil recalls. 'It was a revelation to me that such a work could exist. There and then, I felt driven to write something that would be as compelling. It was as if my whole life before that evening had led up to that particular experience.' Boublil's reaction was to tackle a theme that was, without doubt, the most epoch-making in French history. Shortly after returning to Paris, he proposed to Schönberg that they write a piece of musical theatre on the French Revolution. Both then took the momentous decision to quit their regular jobs to work full time on *La Révolution Française*. It was launched as an album, and as a show, in 1973, with Schönberg singing the part of Louis XVI.

The year of the uneasy lull in Vietnam – 1974 – was a memorable one for Schönberg: his record of his own songs, *Le Premier Pas*, became a bestseller. A possible career as a singer was there for the asking, Schönberg recalls, but he shied away from it. 'It was fun doing Louis XVI at first but it got to be a terrible drag after the first three performances,' he says. 'I felt I was clowning around. The applause was gratifying, but applause helps and encourages the performers, it's for them, not for the composer. I didn't do my work on stage, but at home, in private, at the piano, and applause was of no help at all there.

'These were the years Alain and I started to travel to London and the US to take in musical theatre for the first time. I remember an extraordinary black version of "The Wizard of Oz" [*The Wiz*] and "Pippin".'

The following year, 1975, Boublil and Schönberg were talking, writing and experimenting with a new musical. Set in a never-never-land 'forgotten City' submerged by water, it failed to get off the ground. Like almost everyone else in France that year, they watched the television coverage of the fall of Vietnam with interest and passionate curiosity, but had not the slightest inkling that this might, one day, become the backdrop for one of their own works.

Between *La Révolution Française* and *Les Misérables*, Boublil says, 'we must have worked on half a dozen different ideas, before finally dropping them for one reason or another.' The aborted projects remain unknown, not only because Boublil and Schönberg are extremely secretive by nature where their musical projects are concerned, but because 'we may want to return to one or two of them eventually,' says Boublil. 'The question we constantly asked each other, as we discussed possible themes, was: what is so special about this subject that it simply *has* to be sung? It's surprising how many of them failed the test straight away.' (In musical theatre, all professionals endorse Alan Jay Lerner's famous dictum that 'the most disastrous decisions are taken on day one'.) One of their planned musicals even led to a tentative first five minutes of lyrics and music, but 'it got off to a bad start,' recalls Boublil, 'wasn't working, and was probably a bad idea in the first place.'

'The ultimate sacrifice'

Then, one day, in his Paris home, Schönberg thumbed through a French magazine and spotted a news photograph of a middle-aged Vietnamese woman parting with her child at Tan Son Nhut airport in what was now Ho-Chi-Minh-ville.

'I had no idea how important this simple action would be for me,' he wrote later. 'There was no way I could predict the impact of this photograph. The silence of this woman stunned by her grief was a shout of pain louder than any of the earth's laments. The child's tears were the final condemnation of all wars which shatter people who love each other.

'The little Vietnamese girl was about to board a plane for the United States where her father, an ex-GI she had never seen, was waiting for her. Her mother was leaving her there and would never see her again.

'Behind this particular picture lay a background of years of enquiries and bureaucratic formalities, in order to find the ex-soldier on the other side of the world, with whom that woman had shared a brief moment of her life.

'She knew, as only a woman could, that beyond this departure gate there was both a new life for her daughter and no life at all for her, and that she had willed it.

'I was so appalled by the image of this deliberate ripping apart that I had to sit down and catch my breath. I suffered for the mother as though I might see my own little boy leaving me for ever and I suffered for the child as though in my early youth I had been forcibly removed from my parents. Was that not the most moving, the most staggering example of "The Ultimate Sacrifice", as undergone by Cio-Cio-San in "Madame Butterfly", giving her life for her child?'

The photograph was the real starting point, though at first Boublil was dubious about the validity of a *Madame Butterfly* remake in any form. Then, during a chance stroll along London's Charing Cross Road, close to the Palace Theatre where *Les Misérables* was being transferred, Boublil came across an old, dog-eared copy of Pierre Loti's book, *Madame Chrysanthemum*. In itself, the Pierre Loti book was of no real help to the author-composer team, but both were greatly excited by Boublil's find, regarding it as a favourable omen. 'In a curious way the story had returned to us,' says Boublil. 'It freed us from Puccini, and, at the same time, freed us to write a story that began in Saigon of 1975.'

From then on, Boublil and Schönberg knew that their new project must have both a Vietnam War and a *Madame Butterfly* connection, and – as was their habit – they talked about it, endlessly, before putting any words or music on paper. 'We saw it as our own story retaining the basic Butterfly plot of a misunderstanding between two individuals of highly different cultures, but projecting it into a tragic period of modern history – a time when that basic misunderstanding between two people could reflect the deeper misunderstanding between their respective countries at war.'

'We didn't want a "Pinkerton" type,' says Boublil. 'Instead, we wanted a young man whose life would be instantly transformed by meeting a young girl during the crucial last three weeks of 1975 before the fall of Saigon.' In the course of the talks, they decided on a third character – the Engineer – loosely based on the *Madame Butterfly* character, Goro. Boublil and Schönberg envisaged him from the start as part-French: here was someone they could identify with, whose characteristic French irony and bitterness gave him additional substance. His title came from a 1985 article in the French monthly *Actuel* by Rémi Favret who, in the course of a long piece of investigative journalism about American POWs still believed to be in Vietnamese hands, had interviewed a Thai-based retired French adventurer known as 'l'ingénieur'. Only the name stuck.

'I first got to hear about the new project in the foyer of the Palace Theatre on 4 December 1985, during the party following the first performance of "Les Misérables" after its transfer from the Barbican,' Cameron Mackintosh recalls. 'They cornered me saying that now their new profession as musical writers looked as if it had a future they were glad that they had started to write a new one. Having piqued my interest they then absolutely refused to tell me anything more about the project, not even its name. The more I became impatient at their silence, the more they enjoyed teasing me.'

27

By May 1986, their first draft of the first half of *Miss Saigon* (in French) was ready, and Boublil and Schönberg flew over to London to play it to Mackintosh. 'Cameron had cooked us a lobster in his Montagu Square apartment,' Schönberg recalls. 'Then we sat down and played the tapes, with me singing the lyrics in French.'

'Schönberg hates playing his music live because he never remembers all the notes,' says Mackintosh. 'I was feeling rather tired but as the score unfolded I became wide awake. The style of the music was completely unexpected, very different from that of "Les Mis".'

As Schönberg sang, Boublil provided Mackintosh with a rough translation, 'and I could tell', says Mackintosh, 'that the words were much tougher and more colloquial than before.'

As both Boublil and Schönberg remember that night, Mackintosh's reaction, which was crucial to their project's future, was ambivalent. 'He was clearly totally unprepared for something so completely different, in form and content, from "Les Misérables",' says Schönberg. 'What we had played him was completely unexpected, and he was nonplussed. He said things like: "I don't think I quite understand it, it's bizarre, it's strange, it's terribly dangerous to perform." We left his place with our hearts in our boots, convinced that he had hated it and that he would turn it down.'

'It was not something one could decide on lightly,' Mackintosh explains. 'The subject matter was completely unexpected. It was contemporary, and contemporary musicals don't usually work. It was on a topic that had brought America to the brink, and it was being written about by two Frenchmen. I had to think about it.'

On the plane back to Paris, Schönberg and Boublil were both subdued and apprehensive. 'We were already resigned to Cameron saying no,' says Schönberg, 'and were practically reconciled to the fact.' But two days later, Cameron Mackintosh called. He had played the tapes again and again, he told them, and 'felt we were on to something really exciting'.

'I decided to produce it,' Mackintosh said later, 'despite and perhaps because of the extraordinary challenge it represented.'

4 Pinkerton, Trevor and Chris

As Cameron Mackintosh often says, at the time the project was first brought to him he'd never read *Les Misérables* and even today he can't be bothered to pronounce it properly. For Boublil and Schönberg's next musical, he was better prepared. 'I've seen "Madame Butterfly" a few times,' he admits, 'but I have to say I find it a bit boring. It's a very static opera: parts of it are absolutely wonderful, and sublime theatre music; but for the rest of it I just sit there. I can't get to grips with the characters: with someone like Pinkerton, you wonder why she didn't shoot him in Act One.' In other words, if Puccini, Giacosa and Illica showed up at the Mackintosh office and tried to interest him in the show, they could expect to spend a lot of time shut up in hotel rooms, writing, rewriting and rewriting the rewrites.

Cameron Mackintosh

In the heyday of opera, a good score could cover a multitude of sins, but, in today's musical theatre, you can't buck the 'book' – the dramatic structure on which the music and lyrics depend. For Boublil and Schönberg, the book is always the starting point – as it was for Rodgers and Hammerstein, whose working methods they share. 'Alain and Claude-Michel are essentially musical dramatists,' says Mackintosh. 'They worry away for months and months, if not years, about what the idea is, and finally, when they can't shake it, they go away for three or four months and work out everything *dramatically*, talking through all the lyrics and all the music, before both of them retreat to their various holes to start writing their respective contributions. They work in the same way as Richard Rodgers and Oscar Hammerstein did, as Steve Sondheim does, in that they never use old songs or move songs from show to show.' In this, although they're routinely lumped under the same category of 'British musical', they differ enormously from Tim Rice, who thinks a 'good tune' is its own justification and could work in any number of dramatic contexts, and Andrew Lloyd Webber, who whenever he starts a new show ransacks his own bottom drawer to see what music he has lying around. 'With his big themes, Andrew has a remarkably canny instinct', says Mackintosh, 'of where to place the right melody at the right time. But he's placing melodies he's already put by for the right play. He's rather like someone who finds rare mushrooms in the Dordogne, shoves them in a bag and then knows exactly what to do with them.' Schönberg respects Lloyd Webber's instinct, but would never dream of trying to get away with what the Broadway composer Cy Coleman calls *Eine Kleine Trunkmusik*

29

– going to his 'trunk', pulling out some off-cut from 'Les Mis', and recycling it in *Miss Saigon*. For him and Boublil, each new venture means a fresh start, a completely clean sheet.

'The very first draft is only an outline,' says Boublil. 'We're dealing with Butterfly so we start by relocating a Butterfly-like story in Vietnam, but without knowing where Act One ends and Act Two begins. The second version is a little more precise, but we usually go to a third, fourth or sometimes fifth version, until we end up with what's really a cross between a book for a musical and a movie script. We describe every scene exactly, not only telling the story with all its dramatic connotations, as if we were in the theatre trying to watch it, but also, in our own way, directing it. Of course, we are the worst possible directors, so fortunately, in the finished show, we never see anything that looks like what we'd been thinking of.'

Like all really inspired ideas, *Miss Saigon* seems obvious when you see it in its finished form: *Madame Butterfly* updated to Vietnam; why didn't anybody think of that before? Yet, by any standards, this was a writing assignment which presented all manner of obstacles. 'Pierre Loti's original book is terrible,' says Schönberg of *Miss Saigon*'s source material. 'It's a book of the nineteenth century, written at the height of European colonisation. The Japanese women have no dignity or respect. In "Butterfly" itself, the character of Pinkerton is awful: she is a toy for him, so, when he comes back to the country with his American wife, it is only to pick up the child. There is no problem for him. So we took the basic story of "Butterfly" and, considering that we were writing for 1989, tried to improve the human aspect. We didn't want Chris to be a bastard like Pinkerton – using a girl, leaving her, then coming back. So we changed the story completely – the way they did when "Romeo and Juliet" became "West Side Story".'

In the Boublil-Schönberg version, Chris, a US Marine, meets Kim in a Saigon night-club in 1975 – the final stages of the Vietnam War. They fall in love, but, in the chaos of the American evacuation, are parted. In the renamed Ho Chi Minh City, Kim bears Chris's child – a son whom she intends one day to take to his father in the USA. Like thousands of others, they escape to Bangkok, where Kim, instead of experiencing a joyful reunion with Chris, is introduced to his American wife. With the young Vietnamese girl's hopes dashed for ever, events move inexorably to their tragic conclusion. Although the bones of the original plot remain, the overall mood is startlingly different. Instead of Loti and Luther Long, Boublil began to read contemporary accounts of Vietnam, particularly Michel Tauriac's *Jade*, Olivier Todd's *Cruel Avril*, and John Pilger's *Heroes*, books which paint a vivid picture of Saigon's suffocating humidity and its acceptance of its fate.

Some characters transferred themselves with ease. 'Cio-Cio-San was a geisha, so it was obvious that, in Vietnam, she'd be a bar-girl,' said Schönberg. 'Goro is the transition between East and West: in the opera, they used to dress him in Eastern clothes but with Western hat and shoes. We made him the Engineer. It was not our decision to make him so important, it was the decision of the character himself. He was making everything work: the Engineer became the engine of the show, so we had to have him. Some characters are stronger than you are, they impose themselves on the writing of the book. It was only when we'd finished writing that we realised it was a wonderful part for somebody.' The Engineer, a slippery pimp servicing the Marines' needs with Mimi, Gigi, Yvette, Yvonne and other shop-soiled princesses, runs a bar in Saigon called Dreamland. In between his exhortations to 'check it out, check it out', he provides a cynical commentary on the French, Americans, Communists – the wider landscape against which Chris and Kim's love story is set.

Other metamorphoses were less straightforward. 'The opera had never solved the problem of Kate Pinkerton,' Boublil explains. 'Puccini said he could never find a way to give her a song of her own, he just wanted to get rid of her. We had the same difficulty but we ended up making her a real part, and giving her a proper song.' As some roles were amplified, so others were eliminated or amalgamated. The Bonze, Cio-Cio-San's uncle, and Prince Yamadori, a Japanese who wants to marry her, were combined into the character of Thuy, a Vietnamese to whom Kim has been betrothed since the age of thirteen. Sharpless became John, Chris's drinking buddy who, until a fairly late draft of the script, was a foreign reporter:

> *Engineer:* Ah, Mr John,
>   How's the newspaper game?
>   Still writing lies?
>
> *John:* Yeah, it's always the same.
>   My boss at home
>   Thinks we'll still win the war.
>   He never prints
>   What I write any more . . .

Musical books, however, deal in a kind of shorthand: John's journalism was an interesting diversion, but it was still a diversion. And, as musicals progress through numerous drafts, they become tightly streamlined. Somewhere along the way, it was decided that John would be a more useful character if he had a job in the Embassy – that way, he would be the one who'd arrange Chris's leave with Kim; he'd also be able to take part in the crucial Act

Two scene, the US evacuation of Saigon. So, for sound functional reasons, John became a Marine.

Still, at least he kept his name – if only because 'John' conveniently rhymed with 'Saigon'. For his Western characters, Boublil had simply borrowed the names of his friends in England. 'John' came from John Caird, co-director of *Les Misérables*; Chris was originally called 'Trevor', after Trevor Nunn, the celebrated 'Les Mis' co-director; and Chris's American wife took her name from Nunn's wife, the actress Sharon Lee Hill. Boublil's American friends pointed out that you could trawl dozens of US cities without finding a single Trevor and, if you ever did come across one, you could bet your life he wouldn't be a jaded, drug-happy Marine from Atlanta. As for 'Sharon', her name was quietly changed to Ellen.

These are details, admittedly, but they're by no means unimportant. From the outset, Boublil and Schönberg knew that, on this subject above all, any deficiencies in their understanding of the American vernacular would be cruelly exposed. 'I read an article in New York', Schönberg remembers, 'in which the journalist said that any artist dealing with the Vietnam War has to justify himself before the American audience. Well, we were going to put Vietnam on stage, with people singing and dancing. We knew it was a danger but, like Cameron, we enjoy working with a sense of risk.'

Boublil and Schönberg's particular strain of musical increased the risk: where the Broadway musical has always been credited with a certain naturalism, the 'through-composed' musical – no dialogue – has been most successful when it's dealt with relatively distant period subjects like *Les Misérables* and *Phantom of the Opera*. 'Claude-Michel only wants to write this kind of show,' says Cameron Mackintosh. 'He and Alain aren't comfortable working with chunks of dialogue, although they can just about cope with a few lines here and there – as indeed Andrew did in "Phantom". But Andrew isn't comfortable writing music with dialogue, either. It's the way they are. It's the only way they want to write.'

Twenty years ago, Boublil was in New York and decided to look in on *Promises, Promises* – a perky musicalisation of the Billy Wilder film *The Apartment*, with songs by Burt Bacharach and Hal David and a book by Neil Simon. 'I was bored to death until "I'll Never Fall In Love Again", which was a song I'd adapted in French for a pop singer. And I thought, Why do I have to sit through all this boring dialogue just to get to that song?' Today, Boublil thinks he'd appreciate more what Neil Simon was trying to accomplish, while his composing partner doesn't rule out the possibility of a Boublil-Schönberg musical with dialogue. 'I don't know,' he shrugs, 'maybe one day we'll write one. But, if they're

Alain Boublil

going to talk, it's got to be for a good reason. What I don't like at all is when you don't know why they've started singing or why they've started talking; they can say the same thing talking or singing – it doesn't seem to make any difference. That's why, for me, the best example of that kind of show is "A Chorus Line": there are good reasons for when they sing and when they talk.'

Schönberg's objections to conventional song/dialogue musicals revolve around those potentially awkward gear shifts from one to the other, when you can very easily lose interest in the content because you're too aware of the form. 'It's like when I'm watching a movie, even by the greatest directors, and suddenly I see a light reflected in the car windscreen or on sunglasses. I realise that it's the camera, and it disturbs me for the next ten minutes. I have to concentrate in order to get back to believing in the movie.'

It's a mistake to assume, though, that, simply because there's no dialogue, Boublil and Schönberg don't write books. A few months after *Miss Saigon*'s opening, I chaired a seminar with Boublil, Schönberg and Tim Rice on the merits of through-composed musicals vs. book musicals – a division which the two Frenchmen were most reluctant to accept. They had, after all, won the 1987 Tony Award for Best Book of a Musical. The only difference between their work and the conventional Broadway musical is that the book is *sung*, thereby eliding the distinction between dialogue and lyrics. But, that aside, Boublil and Schönberg are squarely in the tradition of mainstream musical theatre. 'They're not Parisians,' Mackintosh points out. 'They're good Jewish boys – like most writers of the theatre. They're in the new tradition of European Jewish writers, which is after all where most of the American musical theatre comes from.' None the less, if Boublil and Schönberg *are* the successors to Romberg, Friml, Kern and Rodgers, they were at this time still largely unaware of their inheritance. Mackintosh gave them the scripts of both *The King and I* and *South Pacific*, and sent them off to see a London revival of the latter. 'You must see it', he told them, 'because the jumping-off-ground for Rodgers and Hammerstein was "Madame Butterfly".' After poring over *The King and I*, an enthralled Boublil said to Mackintosh, 'As much as I admire him, Stephen Sondheim is not my world. *These* are the sort of English lyrics I would aspire to write.'

Faced with that old question, 'Which comes first, the words or the music?', Richard Rodgers developed a good answer: 'The contract,' he'd reply. In fact, a more truthful answer would be, 'Neither. It's the dramatic situation.' As for Rodgers and Hammerstein, so for Boublil and Schönberg. 'We decide that we are going to have a scene with GIs drinking, talking to each other and the bar-girls,' says the composer. 'Because we've known each

Claude-Michel Schönberg

33

other for more than twenty years, there's no misunderstanding. We have the same vision, so when we agree that that's a good scene to write for the book, *Voila!* My thoughts on the song are exactly the same as Alain's, so he's not going to be surprised by the structure that I give to the music, because we have described in the book exactly what's going to happen onstage, because we know the story from a thousand angles – from above, behind, below, on the side. Sometimes I can be wrong because I don't give Alain enough music for what he has to say, or I give him too much music. But I'm usually not wrong about the atmosphere.'

This system works so efficiently that the writers are even able to plot in the reprises, even though at that stage not a note of the melody in question has been written. 'Even in the book, Alain and I know we have to have a reprise because it is so obvious. We know she has to sing a reprise of the first song, even though it doesn't yet exist, because the situation demands it.'

Apart from the music, though, there is also what Boublil calls a 'lyrical score', with its own themes and motifs, recurring, inter-weaving and underscoring with the same discreet calculation as Schönberg's melodies. 'The show is about West/East, male/female, materialistic/fatalistic,' says Boublil, 'and I mix those elements in exactly the same way the composer does with the music.' As he began work on the book, he realised that he himself also embodied the conflict at the heart of the drama. 'I was more attracted to Kim, I was putting my own words into her mouth, rather than Chris's or the other Occidental men's. Then, when I started to read books about Vietnam, I realised that I had been hiding inside myself. I was born in Tunisia, a country as fatalistic as Vietnam. But I went to France, and became a Frenchman, well travelled, at ease with French culture. Only when I began writing the show did I realise that it had not in any way killed my basic nature, that the country where I was born and its incredible fatalism are still buried deep within me. That's why I was very much at ease with the dichotomy in the show, between the fatalistic Oriental side and the material-istic Occidental side.' It was a dichotomy which the authors believed should cleave all the layers of the show – book, lyrics, orchestrations.

By now, Boublil and Schönberg had been working on the project for eight months, yet they still had no title for it. 'We could have called it "Vietnam!" or "Engineerland" or whatever,' Boublil remembers, 'but it was really just "The Show We Are Doing".' In musicals, a title is vital – which is why so many Broadway shows add an exclamation mark to their names to impart an enticing air of entirely bogus excitement. Sometimes a hit title is all a show has going for it: a lame high-finance musical survived the 1967 season purely on the pulling power of its droll name,

How Now, Dow Jones. But a title is important for more than commercial considerations. It can give the show its focus, define its style. Boublil had been slightly frustrated by his first two projects, *La Révolution Française* and *Les Misérables.* After all, what can you do? It would be perverse to the point of madness to discard names of such proven potency. But he'd always envied Tim Rice for the way he'd managed to find a fresh, unforgettable title for one of the oldest stories around: *Jesus Christ Superstar.*

The solution came when Boublil recalled an old ambition of his. 'I had always wanted to have a beauty contest in a show, like one of those big American pageants. But I always saw it as cynical or ironic. So, one day, this idea came back into my mind, and I said: But the Engineer could have invented a beauty contest; it would be his sleazy perverted version of what the Miss America pageant is. By thinking of that, the title came to my mind immediately.' Boublil dialled his partner's number and said, 'What do you think if we make the bar a kind of cabaret where they have a beauty contest, and we call it "Miss . . ."' Instantly, Schönberg jumped in and anticipated Boublil's title: '. . . Saigon.'

Although *Miss Saigon* is a through-composed musical, Boublil and Schönberg keep the recitative passages to a minimum. Kurt Weill used to say that audiences didn't want 'Would you like a cup of coffee?' set to music, and, too often in the modern musical, composers fall into the trap of setting conversational inconsequentialities to their biggest themes. In *Aspects of Love*, not only is 'Would you like a cup of coffee?' set to music, but so also are requests for armagnac, brandy, a glass of House white and any number of other beverages: there are more drinks ordered in the libretto than during the interval. In contrast, in *Miss Saigon*, the authors tried to impose a song structure on the story. 'When we start,' says Boublil, 'we want to have a theatrical rhythm to the whole piece, but at the same time Claude-Michel and I come from the world of pop song writers, so there are moments for us which can only be songs in the normal sense.' 'But even though it's a song,' adds Schönberg, 'it will be there for a dramatic reason. We don't like the kind of song that stops the action to describe the situation: "How Wonderful Is This Night" or "How Painful I Am". We always try not to do that. We try to keep the action going even inside the song.' In that respect, *Miss Saigon*'s dramatic structure is deceptively simple: a complex story told in song form. Even that smoochy dance tune 'The Last Night Of The World' propels the drama forward:

> On the other side of the Earth
> There's a place where life still has worth.
> I will take you . . .

Almost imperceptibly, Chris has let us know that he will take Kim back to the United States as his wife.

Schönberg is not opposed to recitative, but he doesn't treat it as musical wallpaper or mere text-setting. 'In terms of structure,' he says, 'if I have been influenced by anybody, it is Jacques Offenbach and "Tales of Hoffmann". In the recitative are treasures of melody which are never heard after that. Other composers would have built complete scenes on those melodies, but he used them only for a few bars. I was always fascinated by his ability to write very melodic recitative. And I have to say, in "Les Mis" my favourite parts of the show are in the recitative, and not the main themes.'

Although he waits for the completion of the book before embarking on the score proper, Schönberg usually has two or three melodic themes which begin to bubble around in his mind while he and Boublil are laying out the structure. At the same time, lyric ideas are starting to emerge from the hundreds of scraps of paper on which Boublil has jotted down odd phrases or potential titles. 'I had to find a language for Kim,' says the lyricist, 'and I decided early on to make it a bit mystical and obscure.'

> You are sunlight and I moon
> Joined by the gods of fortune . . .

'In the Buddhist religion,' Boublil continues, 'the sun means the male and the moon the female. So, when we talk about the sun meeting the moon in the sky, it symbolises the union of those human beings in Vietnam. That's why the big celebration in the show is held on the feast of the moon. It doesn't just mean (as it would in America) a romantic evening, it means that that day is blessed. That's very important. In countries like the one where I come from, there are days when, because of the moon principle, the woman becomes impure.'

Musically, it also became clear early on that, apart from the anthem to the *bui doi* (the Unicef song, as it became known), most of the melodic purity in the score would be confined to Kim. 'It's because of her character,' Schönberg says. 'You couldn't give the Engineer a beautiful melody, because he has no purity in his character. It's only a matter of expressing in music the feeling we decided to put in the book.'

By now, the material had come a long way from Belasco and Puccini. In *Madame Butterfly*, Pinkerton demonstrates his contempt for Cio-Cio-San almost from curtain-up, inviting Sharpless, the US Consul, to join him in a toast to his 'real' – in other words, American – wife of the future; in *Miss Saigon*, Chris meets Kim, they go to her room, and, in the morning after, sing a luminous love duet.

According to Schönberg, 'Cameron views the writers as the most important people on a musical, because they are its basis.' But the quid pro quo of that exalted position (which by no means all producers share) is that Mackintosh feels free to point out deficiencies in their work and demand some improvements. After hearing the original demo tape, he felt there was something missing at this moment in the drama. 'Look,' he told them, 'in "Les Mis", the first time we met Fantine, you gave her "I Dreamed A Dream". We need something like that at this point. As we have only got half an hour to set up the love affair, we need to find out what state of mind he's in. We can't go straight into that duet.' The writers chewed this over and came up with a number called 'Why, God, Why?' This first version was dismissed by Mackintosh as 'too Barry Manilow', but, second time around, they got it right. In the early hours of the morning, while Kim lies sleeping, Chris stands alone at the window:

> Why does Saigon never sleep at night?
> Why does this girl smell of orange trees . . . ?

As the end draws near in Saigon, poor burnt-out Chris, reeling through the nights of drugs and booze and whores, has found a moment of intense emotional integrity:

> Vietnam,
> You don't give answers, do you, friend?
> Just questions that don't ever end . . .
> Why me? What's your plan?
> I can't help her – no one can.
> I liked my mem'ries as they were
> But now I'll leave rememb'ring her . . .

Dramatically, it's such a major statement for Chris's character that you wonder how the authors could ever have missed it. 'In the early stages of work', says Boublil, 'you work on the action and try to tell the story. The moments of reflection do not seem very clear until someone else comes from outside and says, "Well, we don't know who this guy is. He doesn't have any serious existence." You need a spectator to the work to come and tell you that.'

If the first version was 'too Barry Manilow', the release of the finished version has overtones of Jim Webb, writer of such Sixties hits as 'MacArthur Park' and 'Up, Up And Away'. In sharp contrast to the broad legato sweep of the main theme, it bustles with a dramatic pop feel, as Chris pushes through the throng of Vietnamese peasants:

> When I went home before
> No one talked of the war.
> What they knew from TV
> Didn't have a thing to do with me.
> I went back and re-upped.
> Sure, Saigon is corrupt.
> It felt better to be
> Here driving for the Embassy.

This is one of my favourite sequences in the whole score, yet it illustrates perfectly the influence of Offenbach's 'melodic recitative' style on Schönberg. Most composers would work it up into a full song in its own right; in *Miss Saigon*, it remains a fragment, which bursts effervescently into the ballad and then recedes for ever.

In that sense, the song's construction mirrors the show's: a blissful love affair blown up by the war. 'It came to our minds immediately', says Boublil, 'that these two people were living in short cut what these two countries – Vietnam and America – had been living. It took time to find the words to explain it, but the metaphor existed from day one.' It adds an extra dimension to the *Butterfly* story, a dramatic backdrop which heightens the personal romance at its heart. But, throughout the writing, Boublil and Schönberg never made the mistake of letting the background take over. 'It's not a history of the Vietnam War,' emphasises Schönberg. 'It's the story of two people lost in the middle of the war.' 'What Alain and Claude-Michel brought me', says Mackintosh, 'was a classic tale of tragic self-destruction, which actually has nothing to do with Vietnam. I would have felt exactly the same if Rodgers and Hammerstein had brought me "South Pacific" – a love story set against the background of World War II.'

Still, even keeping the war in the background, Boublil and Schönberg could not avoid evaluating the Americans and their actions. 'That's what fascinated me,' says Boublil. 'The more I read, the more I was in admiration of America's innocence and naïvety. Other races hide behind politeness – they say one thing and then do what they want to – but most Americans really did approach Vietnam as if it was a good deed.' Boublil was obviously more generously inclined than Puccini, whose use of 'The Star-Spangled Banner' as a personal motif for Pinkerton indicated explicitly that he thought the ghastly Naval Lieutenant was a pretty typical American.

'We improved the plot,' says Schönberg. 'Chris is not a bastard deceiving a Vietnamese girl. He is really in love, he wants to take the girl with him, but the war proves stronger than he is. We were very specific not to introduce a terrible capitalist American fighting the good people of Vietnam. Nobody can say we are either pro- or anti-American.'

Even so, on an issue which many in the US still feel sensitive about, it clearly made sense to enlist at least one American on to the creative team.

Production conference

5 *The Curtains Open*

'Each time I sit down at the piano,' says Claude-Michel Schönberg, 'it's like sitting in the theatre. If the curtains open and I can see something in my imagination, I'm sure the music is going to follow. I write chronologically, so I started on the first day, thinking about GIs dancing and singing and going to night-clubs, and, at the moment when the Engineer goes "*Allez, allez*, welcome to Dreamland," I say to myself now we must listen to something.'

> What are you doing there, John?
> I got ten bucks on Yvonne.
> We should get laid or get drunk
> Since the end is so near . . .

'I didn't fight it. I didn't say it's too jazzy or too rock'n'roll. I knew that, being a different story in a different place in a different century, it was going to be a completely different score from "Les Mis".' For Cameron Mackintosh, though, hearing those opening bars for the first time, it still came as something of a shock to discover the huge gulf between *Miss Saigon* and its predecessor. 'Whereas the word you use with *Les Misérables* is "sweeping",' he suggests, 'the word for Claude-Michel's score here is "restless".' It's a restlessness tinged with foreboding and caught in Schönberg's falling whole tone motif, heard first in the overture, then used as a musical punctuation or underneath stray lines like the Engineer's 'Hey, hey, hey!' or Kim's 'That marine wants his beer.' The first of several Puccini touches, it's reminiscent of a similar device in *Tosca*.

'I realised, talking with some friends,' says Schönberg, 'that as the Vietcong got nearer and they knew they were close to the end, the more the American soldiers in Saigon enjoyed themselves. I wanted to give to the music a sense of that pressure, that all these people were on a volcano, running ahead of the danger. So, from the beginning, there was a general atmosphere to the music.'

At the beginning, however, that atmosphere was only imprecisely sketched: the score was a long way from the full orchestral and choral versions heard in the theatre every night, and little more than an early staging post on the long journey from Schönberg's internal auditorium to the real orchestra pit of Drury Lane. For the composer, though, nothing matches the moment of creation, the moment when a song like 'I Still Believe', Kim's soaring pledge of faith in Chris, first sparks into life. 'It came one afternoon, and I knew it was the right melody for the right situation. And in my head at that time it was perfection, with wonderful voices, a wonderful orchestra, and I know it's never going to be exactly right again. One of my dreams is to have a machine with a helmet on my head that would write out on a piece of paper – you know, like a heart monitor – everything I hear in my brain, perfectly.'

Until the invention of such a device, the process is rather more laborious. For one thing, Schönberg does not notate: he can *hear* the music in his mind, he can play it on the piano and record it on a cassette machine; but he can't write it out. While this would have struck, say, Puccini as an embarrassing gap in Schönberg's education, on Broadway it's by no means unusual. For every Leonard Bernstein, there's a Bob Merrill, writer of shows like *Take Me Along* as well as such infuriatingly catchy songs as 'How Much Is That Doggie In The Window?', a composer who taps out his melodies on a toy xylophone; for every Kurt Weill, there's an Irving Caesar, lyricist of *No, No, Nanette*, who composed 'If I Forget You' by whistling the tune while a secretary took it down, and was so taken by its success that he then whistle-composed an entire cantata, which was rather less successful. Not surprisingly, to those who've undergone years of rigorous conservatory training, these sorts of working methods barely qualify as 'composition' at all. But perhaps the best riposte to that is something Jule Styne, composer of *Gypsy*, once told me: 'Listen,' he said. 'Anyone can tell you how to put notes on paper or the rules of harmony or how to orchestrate, but no one can teach you how to come up with original melodies.' In the early days of the Broadway musical, Victor Herbert once tried to get Irving Berlin, another composer who couldn't put his music down on paper, to take composition lessons, insisting that if he wanted to develop his talents he'd need some formal training. Berlin stuck it for two days before he wised up. 'That sonofabitch,' he said. 'Instead of doing this, I could be writing songs.'

Miss Saigon contains a lyrical echo of Berlin when the Engineer, paraphrasing 'God Bless America', dreams of escaping to the New World ''cross that ocean white with foam'. But there are more important ties between the French composer and his Lower East Side predecessor. Like Berlin, Schönberg has an uncanny ear for harmony, as well as for orchestral detail. 'I can't read music, so I'm really an amateur. But I know exactly what I want, and nobody is going to change one note of the music, one chord, one single voice in the choir without my approval.' Few show composers have managed to retain the degree of control exercised by Schönberg. All too often, they languish helplessly, as the score is taken over by orchestrators, dance arrangers, vocal arrangers, musical directors and, in the era of amplification, sound engineers.

The most important of these is the orchestrator, the man responsible for taking the composer's piano score or lead sheets (just the top line – the 'tune' – and chords) and translating them into a multi-coloured orchestral portrait. For much of this century, it seemed as if every big musical was orchestrated by one man, Robert Russell Bennett, who was responsible for *Rose Marie, Showboat, Oklahoma!, Annie Get Your Gun, Kiss Me Kate, The King And I, My Fair Lady, Camelot* . . . Even after Bennett's retirement, most shows still operated within the 'Broadway sound' he helped create – and which in retrospect perhaps led to the *music* of musicals developing a certain homogeneity. Since then, the leading orchestrators have carved up Broadway into spheres of influence: Jonathan Tunick has spent most of the last twenty years handling whatever Stephen Sondheim has put his way, from the eternally waltzing *A Little Night Music* to the minor modal *Pacific Overtures*; Ralph Burns specialises in brassy, sassy musical comedies like *Sweet Charity* or *Chicago*, the first guy you'd run to for 'Hey, Big Spender!' but not someone you'd be likely to call for *Phantom of the Opera*.

Initially, Boublil and Schönberg had planned to première *Miss Saigon* as a concept album, and turned for the orchestrations to their collaborator on *Les Misérables*, John Cameron. But, after listening to the first rough tapes, Mackintosh felt that it would be 'premature' to reveal the score in this way and aborted the album, at a cost of £185,000. When the record disappeared, so did the orchestrator – for a variety of reasons. I'd never met him, but Herbert Kretzmer introduced us at the first night of *Miss Saigon*: 'Do you know John Cameron?' he asked. 'I'm the one they sacked,' added Cameron, helpfully if a touch lugubriously.

'It was crucial,' says Mackintosh, 'that the musical sound had the same dramatic intensity as the story – just as the orchestrations to "West Side Story" stand up as fresh as the day they were written. I've always been impressed at the time Andrew Lloyd Webber spends building up levels of orchestral textures on his scores. For "Les Mis", we had a recorded version on which to build. Here, we were starting from scratch, and we knew that that concept album wasn't where we wanted to go.'

It is, though, easier to know what you don't want than to find what you do. 'I met one American orchestrator,' says Schönberg, 'and he made me listen to some stuff. It was very very Broadway, and I hated it. That's the last thing I want my music to be.' Cameron Mackintosh turned for advice to Jonathan Tunick, who told him, 'Look, there's this one guy I've worked with a lot. He's only done a few Broadway shows and none of them has been a success. But he has a wonderful knowledge of symphonic sound. I believe he can do this.' Tunick picked up the phone and called William D. Brohn in Connecticut.

'I never found out why John Cameron hadn't been suitable,' says Brohn, 'although I touched upon the subject several times with Claude-Michel and Alain and got a variety of signals, from "I don't want to talk about it", to "We're going in a different direction". As for myself, it was a recording of something I did for Steve Sondheim that really sold me to them. It was a suite of dances from "Pacific Overtures", and Claude-Michel was amazed that he found it so approachable.' Apart from anything else, the *Pacific Overtures* suite indicated that Brohn was at ease with the musical Orientalisms *Miss Saigon* would require.

He is, however, not much of a theatre-goer, and had heard *Les Misérables* only on record, so he kept an open mind until he got home and heard Schönberg's demo tape. His sister was staying with him at the time and, after the first minutes of the cassette, Brohn said to her, 'This is the next breakthrough in musicals.'

William D. Brohn

Singing composers and lyricists are something of an acquired taste. As Alan Jay Lerner used to say of his own vocal technique, 'I'm a democratic singer. I give every key a break.' Most people – not just the public, but many directors and producers (Mackintosh excepted) – find it hard to tell from a rough demo whether the score's a masterpiece or a lot of drivel. A good orchestrator though, prides himself on being able to see the possibilities. 'You can read the enthusiasm – the *heart* – through the voice of the composer, and also the way he plays,' says Brohn, 'although Claude-Michel is the old piano wrecker from the hills far away, and he's raised the tuning bills in my own apartment in New York to astronomical heights. He's actually quite expressive at the piano, but he pounds the living bejasus out of it. And the way he sings completely hooked me: something very clear resounds about what the heart of this musical is. Then you start to become conscious of the melodies themselves, and you realise he's not just French *chanson*, there's also that Hungarian Jewish side of him, the break in the voice that sings through the centuries. That central European thing really fires my blood. My family thought all along we were pure German, but recently an old aunt on her deathbed – sounds like "Oliver!", right? – told me I was part gypsy; one of the great-grandfathers had told her. I fancy that as a connection to Claude-Michel and his ancestors in Hungary.'

The scene which most excited Brohn initially was no more than a bridging moment: after Chris and Kim's first dance at Dreamland, when she leads him to her room. 'Listening to it, I had an immediate vision of it. I heard the dance-floor fading away with that cheap saxophone, and a string gauze, a veil coming in over it, and leading

43

us right up the stairs with them to her attic. It's "Oliver!" again, isn't it? But also "La Bohème" and all that. The stairs and the garret are so romantic to me. I got a shiver just thinking of it. I knew I could make this moment wonderful.' In the end, there was no staircase, but, otherwise, the staging of this sequence matches almost exactly the spirit of Brohn's vision.

That particular melody – the 'song played on a solo saxophone' – reinforces Brohn's point about Schönberg's demo tapes. When he first thought of the tune, he put it on cassette for Alain Boublil, and, as there was at that stage no lyric, sang 'la-la' over the top – except in the instrumental break, where for no apparent reason he began whistling. 'I'd just come back to Brittany and I'd gone for a swim,' Boublil recalls. 'And from nowhere this title appeared. I had to get out of the pool and find a piece of paper, so that I'd remember it: "*Chante comme un solo de saxophone*". It didn't really make any sense, but it sounded beautiful and I thought it had something really exciting about it.' Schönberg loved the title and said, 'You must have been influenced by my whistling.' At that point in the number, he'd heard in his head a saxophone and that was the sound he'd been approximating.

For Brohn, it was fun to orchestrate: 'It starts with the corniest vamp in the world: "*Bump*-ba-ba-*bump*-ba-ba-*bump* . . . " It reminds me of my high-school dances, so immediately they've got *me* and anybody my age. You almost expect to hear The Shangri-las going, "Doo-wah, doo-wah". But then, having pulled you in, it starts to do its number on you.'

Brohn has not often worked in such an overtly pop idiom. He's scored ballets by Agnes de Mille and Twyla Tharp and movies such as *Endless Love*; he's made albums with Marilyn Horne, Frederica von Stade and other opera singers; but he has to reach back to his adolescent dance-band days for any real experience as a pop practitioner. 'When I listen to the radio, it's almost always *not* rock'n'roll or rhythm'n'blues or what have you. But, when it's used in a dramatic context, I can get into it very heavily.' None the less, when *Miss Saigon* opened, one critic remarked of its raucous rocking curtain-raiser that, for all the talk about these new musicals being 'operas', what sort of opera began with an aria that went 'doo-doo-doo-doo-doo-doo-doo'?

'But what was Verdi doing when he put a drinking song in "Otello" and "La Traviata"?' retorts Brohn. 'Those are rousers, those are toe-tappers. Opera has always been very effective at relating to its audience, going all the way back to Rameau who used court dances because that's what the aristocratic audience would understand. Then Mozart arrived and started to see if he could get away with some street tunes in "The Marriage of Figaro" or the Austrian folk song in "The Magic Flute", where you almost expect him to start yodelling. There are many other examples in opera, but, because they're older than "Miss Saigon", they've become accepted as part of the "stuffy" music. When the curtain goes up and you see the business with the girls in their dressing-room and you hear that music, it's one of the things that makes "Miss Saigon" an opera for our time.'

It was also what sustained the Broadway Golden Age: musical drama in a popular idiom. But, as Herbert Kretzmer noted at the time of *Les Misérables*, in the last twenty-five years American show composers, unlike Lloyd Webber or Schönberg, have proved unwilling or unable to incorporate contemporary pop language in theatre scores. 'Most new musical scores are throwbacks,' says Brohn. 'They're almost dinosaurs. They're perfectly adept at what they're doing, but what they're doing is 1955.'

It seems bizarre to hear so musically literate a man as Brohn espousing these sentiments, but Cameron Mackintosh is more cautious: you shouldn't be stuck in 1955, but you can't be 1991 either. 'At school', recalls Mackintosh, 'I still loved Cliff Richard when everyone else had moved on to the Beatles. And that's served me well since – because the one thing the theatre can't do is be in the vanguard of popular music. I don't think it's a coincidence that Andrew's greatest successes have always been great soaring ballads, timeless in their quality. The most obviously pop score, "Starlight Express", was the only one that threw up no real hits.' In his other scores, Lloyd Webber has been far shrewder, creating a pop/theatre hybrid, which sits well on stage but doesn't have that Broadway 'showtune' sound. *Miss Saigon*'s opening number, with its rocking keyboards has a flavour of its period – 1975 – but it is, Mackintosh insists, '*only* a flavour, in the same way that "South Pacific" has a mere flavour of the South Seas but is really mainstream Richard Rodgers.'

What then is mainstream Claude-Michel Schönberg? To one of his critics, the name conjures what he calls 'overwrought Eighties pop ballads' – which is a pejorative term for those foursquare head-on unashamedly emotional melodies like '*Bui Doi*'. But that's only part of his armoury. In an era when show scores have opted for a deadly dull musical consistency, *Miss Saigon* has a refreshing variety. Schönberg seems to be an astonishingly fertile melodist, happy to throw away tunes most composers would be delighted with. Indeed, sometimes it's taken Boublil's shrewd theatrical instincts to spot the potential in what to his partner was no more than a musical afterthought. For example, the penultimate scene in Act One owes its structure and its place in the show to a fortuitous trip to the bathroom.

'I was in Deauville,' Boublil remembers, 'alone in the hotel writing "If You Want To Die In Bed" – or, as it then was in the

French lyric, "If You Want To Make Old Bones", which means exactly the same thing. At that time, it was just verse, refrain, verse, refrain, verse, refrain. And I'd said to Claude-Michel, "Don't you think this is a bit constipated? It's just a funny song, when it ought to be a moment of theatre. It should explode somewhere." And he'd said, "Maybe. But this is all I have." So I was working on it anyway, when I went to the bathroom and happened to leave the cassette on. And what happened was that Claude-Michel had left on the earlier versions, the wrong versions of the same song, so I heard something which went, "*Da*-da-da-da-da-da-*da* . . . " It was a kind of crazy thing which didn't have a shape, and at the end Claude-Michel had gone, "Eeugh! That's silly." But immediately I heard it I felt that this guy, the Engineer, was going to tell us some truth about himself.' (There is a scholarly monograph to be written on lyricists whose first exposure to their composers' tunes takes place in the toilet: it was in more or less the same position that Alan Jay Lerner first heard Fritz Loewe's melody for the title song of *Gigi*.)

Jonathan Pryce (the Engineer) in rehearsal

Eventually, Boublil turned this musical doodle into the dramatic climax of the Engineer's number:

> Why was I born of a race
> That thinks only of rice
> And hates entrepreneurs?
> Me, I belong in a place
> Where a man sets his price
> And you pay, and he's yours.
> I should be – American . . . !

According to Boublil, 'That made the Engineer a proper figure. Until then he really hadn't had to sing too much. But, because of that section Claude-Michel had left on the tape, we were able to make it not only a song, but a *scene*.'

That's something Boublil likes to do more and more as he and Schönberg proceed. He made the same point with the very next number, the Act One finale, 'I'd Give My Life For You': 'I felt totally dissatisfied finishing the act with Kim alone on stage and that kind of normal pop song. It wasn't striking enough. We had to make it bigger.' Once again, it was a question of connecting the personal tragedy with the larger canvas – the exodus of the boat people from Vietnam. At first, Boublil had reservations about this, worried that it would seem 'horrible and cheap'. Schönberg, though, composed a heart-rending 'chorus of pain', a cry from a people who have been helplessly buffeted by forces beyond their control. As before, what had started as 'just' a song had become a powerful dramatic scene.

In the development of such sequences, you begin to appreciate Schönberg's assessment of himself: 'I am a pop songwriter in love with Italian opera. That's all.' It would be easy to see this wildly enthusiastic instinctive composer as an over-ambitious unschooled tunesmith, but it would be wrong: 'He's harmonically very sophisticated,' says Brohn. 'The last thing in the world I would want is for his music to get an overlay of Debussian or Ravelian harmony. I found out very early that when he hears a pure C major triad, he don't want the sixth in it, folks: no gussying up here. He frequently writes a straight triadic harmony with the wrong bass: "Ah, *Monsieur* John/How'd you like to get rich?" It's a straight F minor but the bass goes from an F to a C sharp, it goes off a bit. But he *hears* that and he wants it. Furthermore, as evidence of how well he hears it, he can play anything he's written in any key.'

Although Schönberg suggested many of the orchestral colours himself, Brohn saw his chief task as bringing to a raw, muscular score elements of 'classical music'. 'It's an inadequate term,' he concedes, 'but I've never found an alternative. My training has been in the sounds that have motivated music as a serious art form for centuries, and Claude-Michel liked that.' For Brohn, *Miss Saigon* was the first show on which he was able to indulge his taste for the grand gesture, rather than eke out what he could from a fifteen-piece pit band.

'Not that Cameron doesn't mind the store,' says Brohn. 'He walked in while Claude-Michel and I were working in New York and said, "Not a man over thirty players in Drury Lane." And Claude-Michel said, "Thirty-*two*." Cameron said, "Fuck you, Claude-Michel. You're only getting thirty because of the size of that theatre."' Mackintosh got his way, but, even allowing for the Theatre Royal's capacity (2,200 seats), thirty is still a huge number for a pit band. Traditionally, the orchestrations come fairly low down on the producer's shopping list. By the time they're heard through for the first time, it's often too close to opening to contemplate any major surgery on them. But, with the 'through-composed' musical, orchestration is even more important, and Mackintosh arranged two complete run-throughs, the first a year before, the second four months before opening – an expense few other producers would budget for. 'I can do orchestration on demand as well as the next guy,' says Brohn. '"Here's the tune; can you have it by tomorrow?" But on this show we never had to do that.'

On most musicals, the composer ends up abandoning large chunks of the evening to other hands, and Brohn had assumed initially that either he or somebody else would be doing the 'dance arrangements', musical sections supplied by the yard to fit the choreographer's requirements. Sometimes, these sequences – the

Waiters' Gallop in *Hello, Dolly!* leaps (literally) to mind – can prove the high point of the evening, but they usually have very little to do with the composer. Although 'The Small House Of Uncle Thomas' in *The King And I* uses a few of Richard Rodgers's themes, it's mostly the work of the dance arranger, Trude Rittman. 'I saw the original from the Library of Congress,' says Brohn, 'and at the top, where you put the composer's name, Robert Russell Bennett had written in his own hand "Trude–Rodgers–Hammerstein". It still falls under the grand rights of Rodgers and Hammerstein, though.' There are no unsung heroes on this score; without saying a word, Schönberg made it known that there would be no 'dance arrangements' – *Miss Saigon* would be *all* his music. 'And,' adds Brohn, 'it's a much more unified piece for that.'

Curiously, neither Brohn nor Schönberg ever felt intimidated by the shade of Puccini. Although Cameron Mackintosh likes to tell of how Schönberg visited the composer's grave and knelt before it hoping that some of the Italian's spirit would seep into his bones, for the most part Schönberg manages to detach his love for *Madame Butterfly* from his work on *Miss Saigon.* 'I am forty-six now, I don't cry a lot,' he says. 'But I must say the arrival of Madame Butterfly on stage in the First Act is one of those rare moments of music which brings me to tears every time I listen to it. And the *more* I listen to it, the more I realise how wonderful it is and that I will never reach that state. But what I did for Chris and Kim's wedding music in *Miss Saigon* was an attempt to match the atmosphere of the arrival of Butterfly.'

When Schönberg first played this scene to him, Brohn's reaction was, 'You're Puccini's spiritual brother.' Not so much because of any specific musical similarities, as the overall mood. According to Brohn, 'There's a delicacy and a naïvety and an almost wounded quality to Kim, which comes through so clearly at that moment, exactly the way it did with Butterfly.' And, as Butterfly's arrival does to Schönberg, so Kim's wedding song invariably makes Brohn cry.

There are other Pucciniesque moments in the show, both in Schönberg's score and Brohn's orchestrations. In 'This Is The Hour', the sequence in which Kim confronts Thuy and vows he will not touch her son, they used a Puccini orchestration technique – having the strings 'double' (that's to say, duplicate the melody) in four octaves. 'He's not the only composer to do that,' explains Brohn, 'but he was the first to do it in opera, with such opulence.'

Sometimes, though, Puccini proved an unreliable model. After the coarser come-ons of Mimi, Gigi, Yvette and Yvonne, Schönberg had intended Kim's first appearance before the horny, hungry US Marines to be a soaring Puccini moment:

I'm seventeen and I'm new here today.
The village I come from seems so far away.
All of the girls know much more what to say
But I know . . .

At this point, the music slowed dramatically:

I have a heart like the sea.
A million dreams are in me.

'It was much too obvious,' says Brohn. 'The music threatened to engulf her, and we just couldn't go that far. It's still slowed down, but now it's manageable – it's to draw attention to Kim, to emphasise that she's not the same as the other girls, a way of saying to the audience, "Hey, listen, why d'you think we've got you here tonight? It ain't because of Marines drinking beer and getting laid. Look at her!"'

Lea Salonga (Kim) at the read-through

To Brohn, Kim's early appearances provide some of the most beautiful passages of music in the show, particularly 'Sun and Moon' and the wedding scene. 'Unlike, say, Sondheim, who likes to dig into the complication of every situation, Claude-Michel is not afraid to tackle those moments head on. He feels them sincerely and tells them with musical sincerity. It's very necessary for a through-composed musical, as much as a lyric opera, to find relatively simple moments which just flow, where the heart is dealt with rather than the story.' As Chris sings:

You are here like a mystery,
I'm from a world
That's so different from all that you are;
How in the light of one night did we come
So far?

'It's the Yang side of the story,' says Brohn, 'the female side. It's one of the few moments of sheer joy and pleasure, a refuge from the storm outside. And God knows, all hell's gonna break loose again any minute.'

6 Bamboo Rock

'Thinking about "Miss Saigon",' says Claude-Michel Schönberg, 'I knew I wanted in the very beginning of the score to hear this clash between two cultures. I said to Bill Brohn that in the first ten bars we must understand that we are East but that at the same time there is some Western influence.'

In this respect at least, *Miss Saigon* was aiming beyond *Butterfly*. According to Schönberg, 'When you listen to Puccini's score, you can hear that he had been studying Japanese melodies, although he was not searching around so much for instrumentation and orchestration. But I know he was working with the wife of the Japanese consul in Italy to get some of the melodies right. In fact, his best achievement in this area was not "Butterfly" but "Turandot".' Even then, it has to be said, there's nothing *that* Oriental about the opera's big aria '*Nessun Dorma*' – which is why it sounded perfectly at home as the theme for the 1990 World Cup in Italy. From the outset then, Schönberg wanted more of a *musical* culture clash than Puccini had been interested in. 'It was always my intention that at the beginning we should hear a very conventional Western philharmonic orchestra, but mixed with plenty of little gamelan instruments; that we should have violins and brass facing gamelans, percussion and gongs.' Or as Bill Brohn puts it: 'Without sounding cartoonish, we wanted to say to the audience, "Hey, we ain't sittin' in Piccadilly Circus or Times Square here, folks." And we knew the orchestra would be the key to that.'

We may not be in Piccadilly Circus, but whether we're actually in downtown Saigon depends on how rigorously fine-tuned your sense of musical geography is. Working on *Pacific Overtures*, Stephen Sondheim said, 'I made the, for me, remarkable discovery that the Japanese pentatonic scale (which is unlike the Chinese pentatonic scale) has a minor modal feeling.' There's an exquisite exhibitionism in those throwaway parantheses: Sondheim revels in his research. But, just as Schönberg's music for the US military doesn't aim for specific reduplications of Hendrix or the Stones, so his music for the Vietnamese remains first and foremost Schönberg – flavoured with a soupçon of fairly general Orientalisms, a pot-pourri equivalent to the Mixed Herbs jar which comes in so useful when you can't figure out whether you ought to use oregano or thyme or marjoram. There's a lot of research underpinning *Miss Saigon*, but its purpose was never authenticity for its own sake. It's an approach similar to Oscar Hammerstein's on his beautiful lyric for 'I Am Going To Like It Here' in *Flower Drum Song*.

Hammerstein wrote his text in the form of a Malaysian poetic pattern, a pantoum. But the resulting song is still Rodgers and Hammerstein first, a pantoum second.

In the same way, the 'gamelan' sounds which Schönberg wanted to hear in *Miss Saigon*'s opening bars are broadly South-East Asian, but more particularly associated with Indonesia than Vietnam, and even more particularly, within Indonesia, Java. A gamelan is an orchestra which includes strings and woodwinds but whose distinctive characteristics are gongs, drums, chimes, cymbals, marimbas, xylophones and metallophones. To Western ears, it can sound very strange. Once, some years ago, I was presenting a classical music radio show and decided to slip in some Balinese gamelan music. The programme director came rushing into the studio ten minutes later, convinced that someone – either a nefarious competitor or perhaps even the KGB – was jamming our wavelengths. None the less, many Western composers have been fascinated by the sound: the appearance of a Javanese gamelan ensemble at the 1889 Paris Exposition, for example, had an enormous influence on Debussy.

The Sitzprobe – the first time that the orchestra and cast get together

Years before *Les Misérables*, Schönberg had spent three weeks in Indonesia and passed much of the time listening to gamelan ensembles. The memory of that sound came back to him when he watched *The Killing Fields*, set in one of Vietnam's hapless neighbours, Cambodia, but using the gamelan ensemble of the University of Sydney. In 1987, visiting Sydney for rehearsals of *Les Misérables*, Schönberg went to the University to examine their instruments. 'I was shown into a big room filled with drums, other percussion, all kinds of gamelan instruments, which I later took to a recording studio to make some "samples" of them to put into the synthesiser. It was from this that I started to think about the orchestration, the colour of the show.'

'Because of my "Pacific Overtures" record,' says Bill Brohn, 'I guess they thought I was the Oriental mavin. But I'm not, so the first thing I did was listen to recordings of some Oriental instruments, and then, at Cameron's expense, I got together a battery of percussion players in New York. Mike Hilton, who plays in the pit of "Les Mis", is married to a Japanese girl, he speaks Japanese, he's become a Buddhist or a Shintoist or whatever it is – and he's a freak on Oriental percussion. So we recorded all these instruments he'd gathered, and we ended up using a lot of those sounds as samples in our synthesiser. Then, Alec Roth at the Royal Festival Hall in London was a terrific help. He has a South-East Asian gamelan orchestra, sort of on permanent view: when you go up from the restaurant, you can see it on the third floor. It's a living museum: people come in, take off their shoes and start crashing away on them. For my audition for Cameron, Alec loaned

51

me some of his instruments, even though a lot of them are priceless.'

'It's not strictly Vietnamese,' concedes Schönberg, 'because we ended up with practically no Vietnamese instruments in the pit. It was a blend of the Far East – of instruments from Indonesia, Japan, all over.' But they did 'sample' (i.e., programme into the synthesiser) a *dan tran*, a plucked plectrum instrument from Vietnam, and also a Vietnamese equivalent of the koto, the long zither which is regarded as Japan's national instrument. 'We also tried to make a resonance of the Vietnamese fiddle,' says Brohn, 'but I'm not completely certain it hits the mark. We're still looking at that. We use it to send a vibrato as Kim is talking about her village':

> Do you want one more tale of a Vietnam girl?
> Want to know I was bound to a man I don't love?
> Do you want to be told how my village was burned?
> Want to hear how my family was blasted away?
> How I ran from the rice field and saw them in flames?
> How my parents were bodies whose faces were gone?

At such open-throated emotional moments, the orchestration has to be so discreetly natural that it virtually passes unnoticed. Too many gamelans and it could easily seem ersatz-ethnic. As Brohn says, 'A little of that goes a long way, and I quickly dissolved it in the broth of my Western musical background. The musicologists may storm my apartment for saying this, but I wasn't concerned about differentiating between a reed flute or a wood flute, or whether it was Japanese or Chinese.' Nor on opening night were many of the critics. Most of us displayed our knowledge of Oriental music by throwing the word 'pentatonic' around pretty recklessly. 'What do you think of the score?' asked one of my fellow reviewers in the bar. 'It's very pentatonic,' I said confidently. 'What does that mean?' he demanded. 'You know – the fifth interval.' 'Fifth interval? God, how long's this show go on for?' So much for the in-depth musical analysis. In fact, the pentatonic scale, built on intervals of a fifth, is typical not only of Chinese music, but also of many Scottish folk songs: the tune of 'Auld Lang Syne' is pentatonic, to name but one.

One instrument Schönberg was particularly keen to deploy was the shakuhachi, an end-blown Japanese bamboo flute which dates back to the fourteenth century. You can with difficulty play a chromatic scale on the instrument, but in the main its strength is an almost translucent purity of sound. Schönberg was adamant that the shakuhachi could never be adequately sampled by the synthesiser; it had to be played live in the pit so that, he said, 'it breathes and comes straight from the heart of the player.' 'We limited the use of the shakuhachi to Kim,' says Brohn, 'to when she is singing, or when someone is thinking or talking about her. The wailing of the Oriental flute comes to represent the sacrifice of the Oriental woman.'

Kim's songs have a beautiful luminous simplicity about them, all the more potent for being so starkly in contrast with what's going on around her. In a way, it wouldn't make sense for the Saigon scenes to be strictly Vietnamese in their instrumentation, since the distinguishing feature of the city is that whatever cultural integrity it once possessed has long since been corrupted and perverted first by the French, then by the Americans. Even the robotic Communist march, 'The Morning Of The Dragon', lacks the grim integrity of true totalitarianism. 'I was guided by Claude-Michel,' says Brohn. 'He remembered seeing a procession in the street where they'd used Chinese percussion and accordions (I guess the French would have brought them there), and he explained that that was the effect he wanted: the orchestra would do what it does, but the percussion and accordions were to be the bones of the number. What made it even harder was that the melody is not one of the pentatonics, it's not ostensibly Eastern in any way. It sounds like it came from Uncle Joe and his crew a little further north and west, as if the people are singing a melody they've been taught but which is still foreign. It's been superimposed on them':

Claude-Michel Schönberg and William D. Brohn

> On silent feet it came,
> Breathing a sheet of flame, it came
> Closing in on its rightful prey,
> Burning a hundred years away . . .

'The Morning Of The Dragon' is a more subtle extension of *Miss Saigon*'s musical logic: melodic purity struggles to maintain itself in this battleground of superpower ideologies; the larger tragedy which engulfs Kim and Chris is played out to the sleazier rhythms of the bars and streets of Saigon and Bangkok.

The most lurid of these are the Engineer's songs, an Eastern travesty of Western pop so plausible I had assumed it was real. Not so, according to Bill Brohn. 'The only Vietnamese pop music I've ever heard has been in a restaurant, where someone's brought some records over, put them on a tape and they play them over and over. I have to tune them out, they're so trashy.' Not that Brohn's alternative isn't, as he himself gleefully admits, 'trashy as hell'. You can hear it at its most delightful when the Engineer makes his furtive escape from Ho Chi Minh City:

> If you want to die in bed
> Follow my example.
> When you see a cloud ahead
> It's time to show your class.
> Hit the door
> Before
> They make a target of your ass.

Six months after *Miss Saigon*'s opening, when I visited him in Connecticut, I found Brohn still enjoying this moment so much that he couldn't resist playing it over and over. 'Now you really see what this operator is up to,' he said. 'He's had this influence of Oriental music, American music, French music, and now he's going to put it all together. That vamp at the beginning has a little Chinese gong going, but it's a kind of funny, trashy rock beat. I just have to put it on again . . . ' He crossed to the CD-player, restarted the track and, as the Chinese gongs struck, chuckled, 'Oh, that's beautiful. It's a piece of trash, but it's beautiful.' It sounds exactly like the sort of local pop record you'd expect to hear in a Saigon bar in the Seventies, but actually Brohn invented it himself. 'I call it "Bamboo rock",' he said with pride, 'and I told Cameron, "We're starting a new style here." Let's just hear that again':

> If you want to die in bed
> Don't care too much for country.
> Hit the open sea instead
> And float there like a cork.
> Uncle Ho – Ho-ho!
> I'll have to call you from New York!

And with that, the blaring brass orchestration rocks to its conclusion.

'I suppose,' thought Brohn on reflection, 'that some Vietnamese might find the idea of 'Bamboo rock' offensive. But, er, I think it's funny.' He grinned. 'And I guess if you can't laugh somewhere in this show you're in big trouble, right?'

7 The Problems Begin

'We were looking for something very different,' says Boublil, 'both in the lyrics and in the music. After all, we were tackling a contemporary subject for the first time. We both knew how it should sound, but wanted no trace of a pastiche of any kind, which would have dated it hopelessly.'

Both Boublil and Schönberg were convinced that *Miss Saigon* should start with the beauty contest. From the start, the question of the kind of music appropriate for this scene arose. What would GIs in Vietnam have been hearing in 1975, and should this be reproduced?

The Miss Saigon contest

'They would have listened to music by The Doors, Jimi Hendrix, that sort of thing,' says Boublil. 'Here we were, trying to make a work which would be even more operatic than "Les Misérables", so we had to have our own substance. That was our first major problem.'

The sound of 'The Heat Is On In Saigon' came from a tune that had been lying dormant in Schönberg's mind for quite some time. 'It was pop-sounding, but it was something else, it was acceptable as a scene-setter without being referential music. We never did listen to any of the records of 1975, and this was deliberate,' Boublil says.

Rather than create an imitation of the music of the Seventies, Schönberg invented something new. 'We needed the modern approach but were determined to make it our own; and we wanted an Asian flavour without falling into the trap of writing a pastiche of "South Pacific". There were in fact two dangers: of starting out "Miss Saigon" with Jimi Hendrix overtones, or as a pastiche of an old Asian-American musical. We had to do it our way, and it was more difficult than anything we had ever tackled previously.'

The other problem was content. 'You're dealing with such a serious subject,' says Boublil. 'When we started on it the war had been over for ten years. There had been some movies about the war, but there hadn't been any so far along the lines of "Good Morning, Vietnam". "Platoon" was still to come. We were in fact pioneering something not knowing that in Hollywood they were planning movies about almost every conceivable aspect of the Vietnam War. The very idea of saying: we're writing an opera about the Vietnam War, sounded absurd.' On the plus side, Boublil recalls, there was no set story, as there had been in *Les Misérables*. 'We could go wherever we wanted to go. This time, we weren't bound by a Victor Hugo plot.'

55

For Mackintosh, however, problems of a very different order were looming. Looking ahead to the completion of the lyrics, he wondered who should direct *Miss Saigon*, and what his production team should be.

'Preparations were meticulous,' he says. 'They were inexhaustible in order to get the material right. But that's very different from trying to make sure one had a saleable commodity. I was embarking on something we all wanted to become a success. Here was a subject gripping the imagination, a wonderful idea, but terribly difficult to bring about. We had to do everything we could to make it work, but at the same time I was driven to *not* make it safe, i.e., palatable. If we had tried to make it palatable I believe it wouldn't have worked. What none of us wanted was another "Les Mis".'

Even before the question of who would direct arose, there was the problem of the English libretto to be solved. For *Les Misérables*, first James Fenton and then Herbert Kretzmer had worked on the English version; by now Boublil's English was perfect, and colloquial, but he knew he needed a collaborator. Without consulting Mackintosh, he flew to London to talk to Herbert Kretzmer.

'Alain stressed he was not making an "official" move,' says Kretzmer. 'He hadn't even told his partner. I listened to a tape of what they had done, in French. Had Boublil said: "We had a great hit, and a great time together, doing 'Les Mis', let's do it again," I wouldn't have had any hesitation whatsoever. But it was clear to me that he wasn't about to make me an offer. What he was seeking was advice.'

Four months later, in a fast-food hamburger joint in New York, while recording the original Broadway cast record of 'Les Mis', Boublil and Kretzmer, with Schönberg this time, talked again about the *Miss Saigon* project. 'It was clear to me', says Kretzmer, 'that Alain wanted to write it himself. It wouldn't be like "Les Mis", where I had done an extensive rewrite virtually from the ground up. What he wanted was someone to work on the areas he found difficult to complete. I believed, from the start, that "Miss Saigon" was a wonderful subject, but I don't think politically, and talked myself out of the assignment as, in the past, I had talked myself out of "Phantom of the Opera". [Herbert Kretzmer had been approached by Andrew Lloyd Webber to work on the lyrics of *Phantom*, but had raised a number of questions about the characters in the musical, urging Webber to make considerable changes which would have delayed production. He was not selected.] I had only the interests of "Miss Saigon" at heart, and wanted them to succeed. I told them: You should have an American who could reach for the idioms instinctively. I'm a South African born resident of London, not a US lyrics writer. You need someone who doesn't have to reach for the words.' Had Trevor Nunn been committed to the project, however, Kretzmer admits that he might have spoken differently.

Unknown to either Kretzmer or Boublil, however, Mackintosh already had his eye on an American collaborator. Richard Maltby, Jnr, a director-lyricist with whom Mackintosh had worked on Andrew Lloyd Webber's *Song and Dance* in New York, was in fact his first and only choice. Mackintosh was puzzled when Maltby turned him down.

Richard Maltby Jnr

What Maltby had listened to was the French tape of the first act, the same tape that had convinced Mackintosh that he should go ahead. 'The melodies were ravishing and the theme daring,' recalls Maltby, 'but my first reaction was: what's going on here? Two Frenchmen, clearly admirers of Puccini, were proposing a modern operatic retelling of the "Madame Butterfly" story in the context of the Vietnam War, a war so damaging that by 1986, the year I was approached, many Americans still didn't want to hear about it. I was already committed to a new show. Embarrassingly, I recall I was not entirely unhappy to use this as a pretext: whoever Boublil and Schönberg were, I thought, they were crazy to embark on this project and I was saving myself considerable grief.'

Over the next few months, Maltby slowly changed his mind. One reason for this was the unexpected success of the Oliver Stone movie, *Platoon*. Another was the compelling sound of the *Miss Saigon* tape, which he played over and over again. Finally, he went to see the Washington production of *Les Misérables*, and was impressed. 'I suddenly saw what Alain and Claude-Michel were up to: nothing less than the invention of a new kind of musical story-telling, combining the impulses of grand opera, American and English musicals, and popular music.' Maltby called Mackintosh to find out whether a final writer assignment had been made. Mackintosh responded by asking him to hear the second act.

The result was an intense, unusual writing collaboration. 'What occurred at first had almost nothing to do with lyrics,' said Maltby. 'We started out by writing a play, developing the characters and dramatic action. Only at the end of the discussion did the dialogue begin turning into lyrics.'

Conventional song-writing, both Maltby and Boublil knew, would not work for *Miss Saigon*. 'We had to find other answers,' says Maltby. 'We devised a language far removed from conventional "musicals" which, we hoped, would be appropriate for this tough, realistic yet still poetic drama.'

Maltby and Boublil began work in 1987, in a Paris hotel room where they were sure they would not be disturbed. Writing continued in Brittany, in Gordes (near Avignon where Boublil has a house), and in America.

57

It's difficult to say what makes a writing team click. Temperamentally, Boublil and Maltby are very different: Boublil is intense, a quintessentially French intellectual with a passion for analysis. He is introspective, serious, with sudden flashes of merriment and irony. A Tunisian-born Jew who only formally became a French citizen long after his student days were over, his intellectual isolation has been compounded by the fact that Paris has not been renowned as a home for musical theatre since the days of Offenbach, and that, apart from Claude-Michel Schönberg, there are few people in France he can meaningfully discuss his work with. A star in Britain and the US following the resounding success of *Les Misérables*, Boublil remains relatively unknown in France, where a mention of the musical *Les Misérables* will almost inevitably provoke the rejoinder: you mean the show staged by Robert Hossein at the Palais des Sports? It is this, perhaps, that has since caused him to settle in London.

Maltby, on the surface, at least, is placid, serene, relaxed. Watching the interplay between him and Boublil (for around this time, I was called in from time to time for background advice, based on my own experience of the Vietnam War) I was struck above all by its easy-going harmony, and the fun the two were having. Lyric-writing involves endless playing with words, which become like bricks in a child's playground, and for all his unmistakable New Yorker one-liners and self-deprecating humour, there were an innocence and clarity about Maltby that, perhaps, are reflected in both the characters of Chris and Kim. What made the team so strong were Maltby's ease with words and rhymes, and Boublil's relentless concern for the story. No matter how brilliant, or how enticing Maltby's juggling with catchy, eminently singable words, Boublil was there to remind him of the need to keep the dramatic pace going, and to avoid anything that might provide a digression from the tale of Kim and Chris. While Boublil was unable to tackle subjects that were not brimming with strong, emotional content and moral significance, Maltby was perfectly at home in the world of the small-scale, almost revue-like off-Broadway musical, and rapidly acquired the idiom of the GI language of the Seventies.

Above all, both Maltby and Boublil had the invaluable quality of patience: both knew, from their considerable experience, that there would be bad moments, discouraging, non-productive days when nothing would seem to work and everything they attempted to put down on paper would appal them with its triteness. There was, of course, a language barrier, since Boublil's original lyrics had been written in French and Maltby's French was virtually non-existent, but culturally both were on the same wavelength, and knew that good lyrics depended not only on slick words, but on the credible behaviour of their characters.

8 A Young Lover and His Mistress

Just before the opening of *Miss Saigon*, it was announced that Cameron Mackintosh had endowed the first Chair of Contemporary Theatre at Oxford University, and that Stephen Sondheim had agreed to serve as Visiting Professor for the inaugural year. It sounded a bit like some hoary old Thirties B-movie – *Musical Comedy Goes to College* – and on Friday afternoons it was, as bemused actors, choreographers and orchestrators arrived at the porter's lodge for the weekly lectures. At one of these, Alain Boublil was surprised to hear Tim Rice, discussing the state of the modern musical, claim that lyrics were now virtually irrelevant: in most producers' pecking order, the lyricist came well below the composer, director and designer and only just above the usherette.

'What Tim was saying is unacceptable to me', Boublil insisted, 'because it comes from the man who wrote "Jesus Christ Superstar", which has some of the most beautiful lyrics in the theatre. It was the show that changed my life. The lyrics had a modernity about them, something I could hope to reach one day.' At that time, Rice and Andrew Lloyd Webber were equals. But, as the composer has turned to other lyric-writers, so the balance has shifted – to the point where, as one of them puts it, they are (in *Madame Butterfly* terms) Giacosa and Illica to Lloyd Webber's Puccini.

Driving with Don Black down to Lloyd Webber's country house to discuss *Song and Dance* with him, Richard Maltby was surprised to see so much traffic streaming away from such a small and remote village. 'Who are all these people?' he asked. 'Lyricists,' replied Black drily. 'Andrew', says Charles Hart, the composer's collaborator on *Phantom of the Opera* and *Aspects of Love*, 'changes lyricists the way other men change their underpants.'

Older writers would probably say, what's new? Lyricists throughout musical theatre history have become famous either by being their own composers (Berlin, Porter, Sondheim) or by being one half of a permanent words-and-music team (Gilbert and Sullivan, Rodgers and Hammerstein, Lerner and Loewe). Today, the economic climate on Broadway being what it is, an exclusive partnership is harder and harder to maintain, and the only exemplars of what Alan Jay Lerner always argued was the ideal working relationship are, on the one hand, Kander and Ebb (writers of *Cabaret*) and, on the other, Boublil and Schönberg. Before *Miss Saigon*, though, Alain Boublil held an even rarer honour. He was one of the few powerful, respected and bankable lyric-writers in the English-speaking theatre, yet not one line of his songs was known to the public. His early work on the new project only emphasised the bizarre niche he occupied: 'For the first time,' he says, 'I had to write the show in French knowing it was not going to be played in French. It was going to go straight into an English theatre.'

Unlike 'Les Mis', this time Boublil had no time to polish his French lyrics. Once Mackintosh had decided to put the show into production, they had to start looking for an English writer. It was then that both Schönberg and Mackintosh began pressuring Boublil to adapt the French text. 'Little by little,' he recalls, 'I had to admit that this was the only solution. I could have been comfortably seated in the censorship chair, saying "I like that, I don't like that." But I felt I had to take the risk.' When the posters went up, even theatre professionals failed initially to notice the subtle difference in the 'Les Mis' and *Miss Saigon* billings: for the first time, Boublil would be writing lyrics in English.

'It must be very frustrating for Alain,' says Cameron Mackintosh. 'According to my friends who speak French, he is a very considerable lyricist – in French. That is what he's been born into, and he can never change that. Whereas Claude-Michel's music is international, Alain is always, for the foreseeable future, going to need a bed partner.' Almost all Mackintosh's metaphors revolve around bed partners: he sees himself as the Dolly Levi of musicals – a producer who puts his creative team together by 'arranging marriages'. 'It took', he continues, 'the very great man that Richard Maltby is to settle for only ever being the mistress of Alain Boublil; the wife was always going to be Claude-Michel – and "Miss Saigon" was their baby.'

You can see what Mackintosh means – even if, in such an extravagantly extended metaphor, it sounds as potentially explosive a triangular romance as that of Kim, Chris and Ellen. As it turned out, it was an agreeably harmonious *ménage à trois* – thanks to the authors' mutual respect and perhaps also Maltby's easy-going nature: 'At our very first lunch, Cameron said, "Alain could *almost* write this, because his ear (like his sense of drama) is good. But not quite yet." I guess he had seen on "Song and Dance" my capacity to sit and work with someone else – and how many other floating lyricists are out there?'

Earlier in his career, Maltby had suffered from what many of his peers have discovered – the sense that, as a lyricist only, you don't have any clout. 'In the Sixties, I was always off in a small hotel room writing the lyrics, while everybody else was in rehearsals having all the fun. I felt powerless. I would write something one way, and then it would go on stage and be different. Then I realised the director had not understood the song: he didn't make it happen and so it had died. So I started to direct myself.' Since then, Maltby has adapted and directed *Song and Dance* for

Broadway, conceived and directed the Tony-winning *Ain't Misbehavin'*, written and directed the 1983 hit *Baby*, all of which, you might think, would make his role on *Saigon* – co-lyricist – seem a trifle restricted. 'I've never worked on a show that hasn't been *my* show from the inception. Once I realised that this was a show from another source that I was *contributing* to, it was a great relief.'

Maltby eventually found an agreeable liberation in being a mere 'contributor' – thanks to a line from Boublil. 'He suggested something and I said, "But how are you going to get from here to there?" He said, "That's a director's problem." I was appalled. And then within the day I thought, "That's right." I remember sitting at the typewriter writing things like, "They go into one floor of the Embassy, they go up a floor, they barricade the door, they go up another floor."' Maltby shrugged his shoulders and beamed: 'Director's problem. I don't give a shit.'

Actually, he did. Whatever his wilfully impractical stage directions, Maltby was never an uncommitted hired hand. Indeed, in one respect, as an American of the Vietnam generation, he was the most personally involved of all – almost painfully aware of every complex contemporary resonance in the subject. Listening to him talk about the war, I wondered whether he didn't wish he'd thought of this musical first. But, apart from the story, Maltby was also attracted by his collaborators. 'One of the things I find so stultifying in American musicals is that everybody knows too much. We know how Rodgers and Hammerstein did it, we know how Cole Porter did it, yet we sort of want to do that moment again, the way they did it. Alain and Claude-Michel have the enthusiasm of discovering it for the first time. When you see them, it's almost like young lovers: they think they've invented it.'

There's a certain amount of truth in that. When he saw *West Side Story*, Boublil liked it enormously, but without being aware that the lyrics were by Stephen Sondheim; he liked Jacques Brel and Charles Aznavour, too, but again as an eager listener rather than a disciple of their lyric patterns. He is, you feel, an instinctive lyric-writer, yet so far his instincts have been remarkably accurate. Even in the original French, for example, *Les Misérables* and *Miss Saigon* demanded completely different lyric styles. 'The vocabulary we are using in English', he explains, 'is exactly the one I expected we would use. When Richard suggests a word I know if it's right or not, because I know English vernacular maybe better than I know French vernacular. The big difficulty for me was to write in colloquial French, because you never use that in songwriting. You use instead a kind of songwriting style. On "Les Mis", you could go into that beautiful language, use a little of Victor Hugo and then make it yours.'

In that sense, *Les Misérables* was squarely in the tradition of

Peter Polycarpou (John) and
Simon Bowman (Chris)

French lyric-writing, which has always preferred a stylised poetic language rather than, as in America, the cadences of everyday speech. Although in the last decade or so certain French rock writers have opted for a more colloquial approach, most of Boublil's compatriots still don't see why lyrics should defer to the emphases of spoken French. They're quite happy to say '*La vie en rose*' but sing '*La vie en ro-ZUH*.' 'French is uninflective,' said Maltby, 'so therefore any beat can be important. But in English only certain beats can be important.'

Meeting Boublil and Maltby after one writing session, I saw some of the niggling problems this could cause. Boublil was very proud of having managed to get in a neat American slang expression at the end of a line: 'big shot'. 'But the music went "Da-*da*",' complained Maltby. 'You can't say "Big *shot*". It's "*Big* shot". Maybe you could do that in French because you can inflect any beat.'

In other words, it has to be a feminine rhyme – 'That big shot/ Had his pig shot' or whatever. 'Presumably,' I asked Boublil, 'you'd rhymed "big *shot*" with "cot" or "dot" or something?'

'Well, I would have liked to,' said Boublil sheepishly, casting a glance at Maltby which indicated he hadn't yet accepted the argument. You can't blame him. After all, as Chris sings in the Engineer's club:

> That little girl, we could be in the sack
> For what it costs me to buy a Big Mac.

If it's 'Big *Mac*', why isn't it 'Big *shot*'? Anglo-American lyric-writing is fraught with such perils, particularly when combined with the distinctly Gallic inflections of Schönberg's music.

'It was difficult for me, too,' admits Maltby, 'because you'd begin to convince yourself something was in the vernacular just because it fits. The big thing for me was always "cannot": "I cannot do this", "I cannot do that", always fits into the rhythm. Well, maybe Kim would say "cannot", but none of the Americans would. They'd say "I can't". It was very easy to fall into the trap of attaching yourself to those phrases rather than trying to find natural English.'

Lyric-writing is a miniature art, so, to its finest exponents, every tiny blemish can seem like the Rock of Gibraltar. It was only after Maltby began analysing the 'cannots' and 'can'ts' in the text that I noticed that Boublil himself, although an excellent English conversationalist, tends to say, 'I cannot'. As a *writer*, however, he understood Maltby's objection. After all, it was a trap he had already negotiated in the original French: 'Kim would have said "*je ne veux pas*" but the soldiers would say "*j'veux pas*".'

'To that extent,' says Maltby, 'the basic impulses in the French text are always discernible in the current version.' According to Boublil, 'Richard taught me that it's never by accident that you have that first impulse. Whenever we were lost, he would say, "Alain, when you first thought of this, why did you put it in?" It helped me understand myself.' Unlike *Les Misérables*, the version of *Miss Saigon* which eventually opened at Drury Lane followed broadly the original French-language demo. Many of the song ideas and lyric thrusts also survived, and some – such as 'I Still Believe' and 'I'd Give My Life For You' – are more or less direct translations.

Curiously, the lyric which underwent the most transformations before reaching its final form was neither French nor English but Vietnamese. For the scene where Kim's and Chris's room is blessed Boublil had used the sort of blessing he'd read in books about Vietnam: 'They were always in French: "*Bonheur à infini*", that kind of thing. That's what I'd used in my first draft, and I kept going to Vietnamese restaurants and asking the waitresses for a translation, and every waitress had a different answer.' So in one version of the song the girls sang: '*Tan djo bac niem hao hap . . .* ' But then, after speaking to another waitress, Boublil produced a new version: '*Ngay tan hon hanh phuc nhieu . . .* ' 'Whether there is a different dialect for each village, I can't tell you,' says Boublil, 'but that might be the case. Anyway, no two waitresses agreed. So finally I decided to stick by one of them and choose the version which made the best *sound*.' In lyric-writing, sound can be as important as sense, and set to Schönberg's Pucciniesque melody the final text is shimmeringly euphonious:

> Kim: *Dju vui vay yu doi my*
> *Dju vui vay vao nyay moy.*
>
> Chris: It's pretty but what does it mean?
>
> Kim: It's what all the girls sing at weddings . . .

The opening number was also substantially altered, though without the expertise of Vietnamese waitresses. Originally, the soldiers, enjoying some R & R in Saigon, had sung about being stuck in the rice-fields. 'When we were working on it,' says Maltby, 'we had a list of fifteen different lines, one of which was "The heat is on in Saigon". And that was the one that Alain responded to, that he thought we could put up at the front and see whether it holds. It was surprising to me at the beginning of the project, when you're just sort of fishing with your collaborator, that a Frenchman would understand all the nuances of that phrase. The heat is on because it's a hot night and it's a bunch of girls; and because there's tremendous pressure on the city; and then there are the police detective overtones of the phrase. Alain picked up on all of that.'

So, from that first tough curtain-raiser, Boublil and Maltby put as much distance as possible between *Miss Saigon*'s lyrics and the grandiloquence of *Les Misérables*:

> The heat is on in Saigon –
> Don't tell me I'm reassigned,
> All that chickenshit sucks.
> Tonight I'm out of my mind,
> Not to mention ten bucks . . .

Richard Maltby, Claude-Michel Schönberg, Alain Boublil and David Caddick (production musical supervisor) at a vocal rehearsal

Cameron Mackintosh is wary of putting individual lyric lines under the microscope. 'There are a few areas which Alain and Richard would be the first to admit are serviceable as opposed to brilliant. But sometimes you can't have everything. The *piece* works. I get irritated with people who say, "Ah, well, it must be rotten because this song has got 'moon' and 'June' in it." They've lost sight of the important question: does the dramatic structure of the piece work? Several great writers have said to me, "Provided the dramatic cohesion is right, they won't notice the odd bad lyric." And they don't. You keep striving for perfection, but in the end one line won't stop the internal motor of the show.'

That said, on a musical with such a cruelly naturalistic contemporary setting, the lyrics have to withstand greater scrutiny than they would on period pieces like *Phantom*. As Stephen Sondheim has said, 'In any realistic terms, the musical is hilarious.' It only requires one clumsy couplet to destroy the conceit: the solemnly descriptive tumty-tumty observations about army life were enough to set the aisles sniggering and put the skids under Howard Goodall's 1987 World War II musical *Girlfriends*. War is messy and the fixed rhyme patterns of theatre songwriting can easily seem too neat, too pat, too organised. Perhaps the greatest achievement of Boublil and Maltby is the way they make the characters and the subject sing so naturally. You never feel the show is in danger of succumbing to what in deference to Mel Brooks we ought to call the *Springtime for Hitler* syndrome: the tendency, when musicals tackle big subjects, of the form to demean the content. Instead, the soldiers' lyrics spit a bleary, battered realism: 'I got the hots for Yvonne/We should get drunk and get laid . . . We lost the war long ago/What is this bug up my ass . . . ?'

For the most part, though, musical theatre deals in certainty. It's never been very effective at grappling with ambivalence, confusion, blurred moral lines. And in America, even after all these years, the war continues to reach out and ensnare in ever more slippery tentacles. To most people, an issue which can lead former draft-dodgers to hail an embarrassed Republican vice-presidential candidate as a hero would seem beyond the reach of the musical. 'On "Miss Saigon",' says Maltby, 'the only big statement that was in my mind was that the love story paralleled in a curious way the American involvement. That is to say, even on a level of one person trying to save one other person, we couldn't do it.'

Despite his description of himself as a 'contributor', it's clear that Maltby did make a difference to the story's perspective: '*we*' couldn't do it. Originally on *Miss Saigon*'s writing team there was no 'we' about the drama. Once Vietnam ceased to be French in 1954, the metropolitan power simply shrugged it off with the insouciance of one of the least idealistic of all European empires. 'I was a boy when we lost Vietnam,' Claude-Michel Schönberg said, 'and I didn't mind at all. After all, we French are always losing wars. The only ones we ever win are when the British and the Americans come in and help us out.'

'There was one area that startled me,' Maltby recalled, 'and that is that neither Claude-Michel nor Alain nor even Cameron really understood how devastating the Vietnam War was to the American psyche. Europeans, you've lost so many colonies, what's the big deal? That was just not an American pattern.' Reading the first version of *Miss Saigon*, Maltby was appalled to discover that Chris was another Pinkerton – 'just an army shit' – and immediately began rebuilding him as an all-American idealist.

'How much idealism would he have if he's been through all of this?' wondered Boublil. 'He's been spending every night fucking his brains out in a brothel, he's done every kind of drug. Would he have *any* idealism left?' Listening to the lyricists argue the toss, you appreciate what an odd couple they make: Boublil is a sceptical cosmopolitan; Maltby at times seems almost the personal embodiment of American naïvety and guilt over Vietnam. As an exercise, Boublil and Maltby wrote another draft, making Chris the ultimate American innocent. 'He was a "real good boy",' said Boublil, injecting the phrase with a touch of sarcasm. 'From the beginning, he says, "I hate all this. I had a good reason, I came here to fight for my country, but I'm here by mistake." I wanted to understand how far Richard could go in believing that this boy was like him when he was eighteen or twenty-two. But Chris is *not* Richard when he was eighteen . . .'

Maltby took the point, and gradually a true Chris began to emerge, neither as cynical as Boublil's first draft nor as starry-eyed as Maltby's. Chris was burnt out, dehumanised, a man who (unlike the draftees of *Platoon*) had returned to Vietnam by choice; yet, despite Saigon's pressure-cooker debauchery and spiritual empti-

ness, he is still capable of genuinely falling in love with Kim. On
their first night together, the Vietnamese girl sings:

> You are sunlight and I, moon
> Joined here
> Bright'ning the sky
> With the flame
> of love . . .

'Sun And Moon', Kim and Chris

When Chris joins in with these romantic sentiments, you believe
him. That's the difference between him and Pinkerton. 'Our hero
is a good man,' says Maltby. 'In the second act, he and his wife
do commit the American crime again, of deciding what's best for
the native girl. But I felt strongly that that should happen. They
can't be let off the hook.'

Maltby is proudest of the hotel room scene in Act Two, when
a bewildered Chris finally spills out his pain to Ellen:

> Christ, I'm American.
> How could I fail to do good?
> All I made was a mess, just like everyone else . . .

The key line for Chris is 'I wanted back a world I knew'. He loved
Kim, but when the war was over and she was shut off from him
in the new Vietnam he needed to rediscover his old life, to free
himself. Boublil and Maltby had found an explanation for Chris's
behaviour that didn't turn him into a Pinkerton.

The day after *Miss Saigon* opened, Richard Maltby flew back to
New York to begin rehearsals for *Closer Than Ever*, a four-handed
revue in a 190-seat off-Broadway theatre. 'From Drury Lane to
the Cherry Lane,' he said cheerily. 'It's not so very different.' Not
many producers would have thought of matching Alain Boublil,
pioneer of a new form of sweeping operatic musical, with a man
who specialises in intimate observational character shows. But, as
on so many other occasions, Cameron Mackintosh's hunch had
proved correct.

Above   Backstage at Dreamland

Following pages   'The heat is on'

'The movie in my mind,
The dream they leave behind'

'You are the first to score tonight'

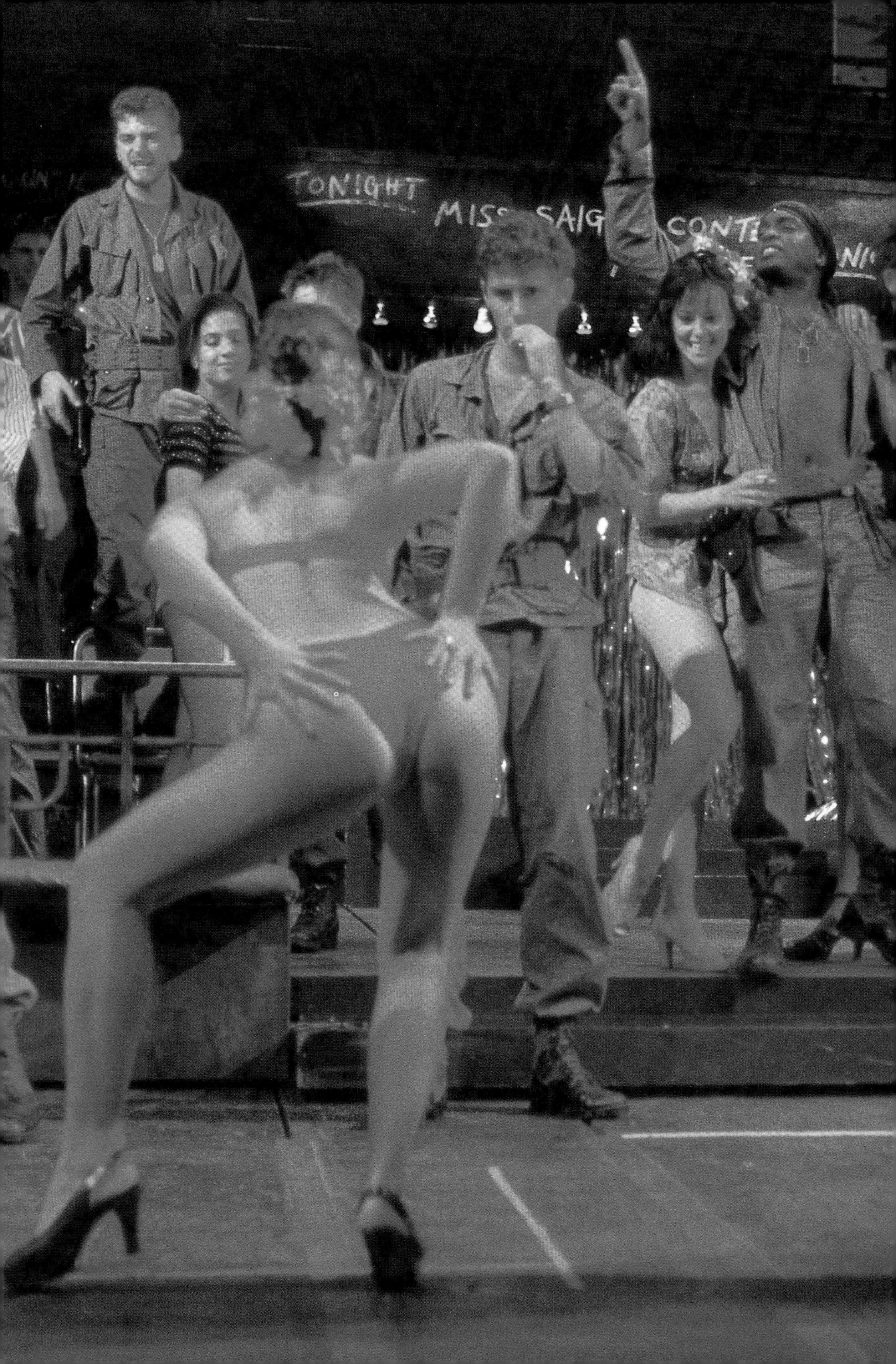
TONIGHT
MISS

Previous spread   The dance

Opposite   'My name is Kim,
            I like you Chris'

Above   'Don't say a word,
            Just come with me'

Following pages   Saigon at night
            'You are sunlight and I, moon'

TAN-SON-NHUT
MACV CIVIL AIR TERM
PHONG
NGHIA TRANG BAC VIET
36
PHONG

Above   'We have been blessed, you and I'

Following pages   '*Dju vui vay yu doi my*
Dju vui vay vao nyay moy'

'You broke your father's word,
This is your curse'

Above   'So stay with me,
          And hold me tight'

Following spreads   'The Morning Of The Dragon'

          'On silent feet it came,
          Breathing a sheet of flame'

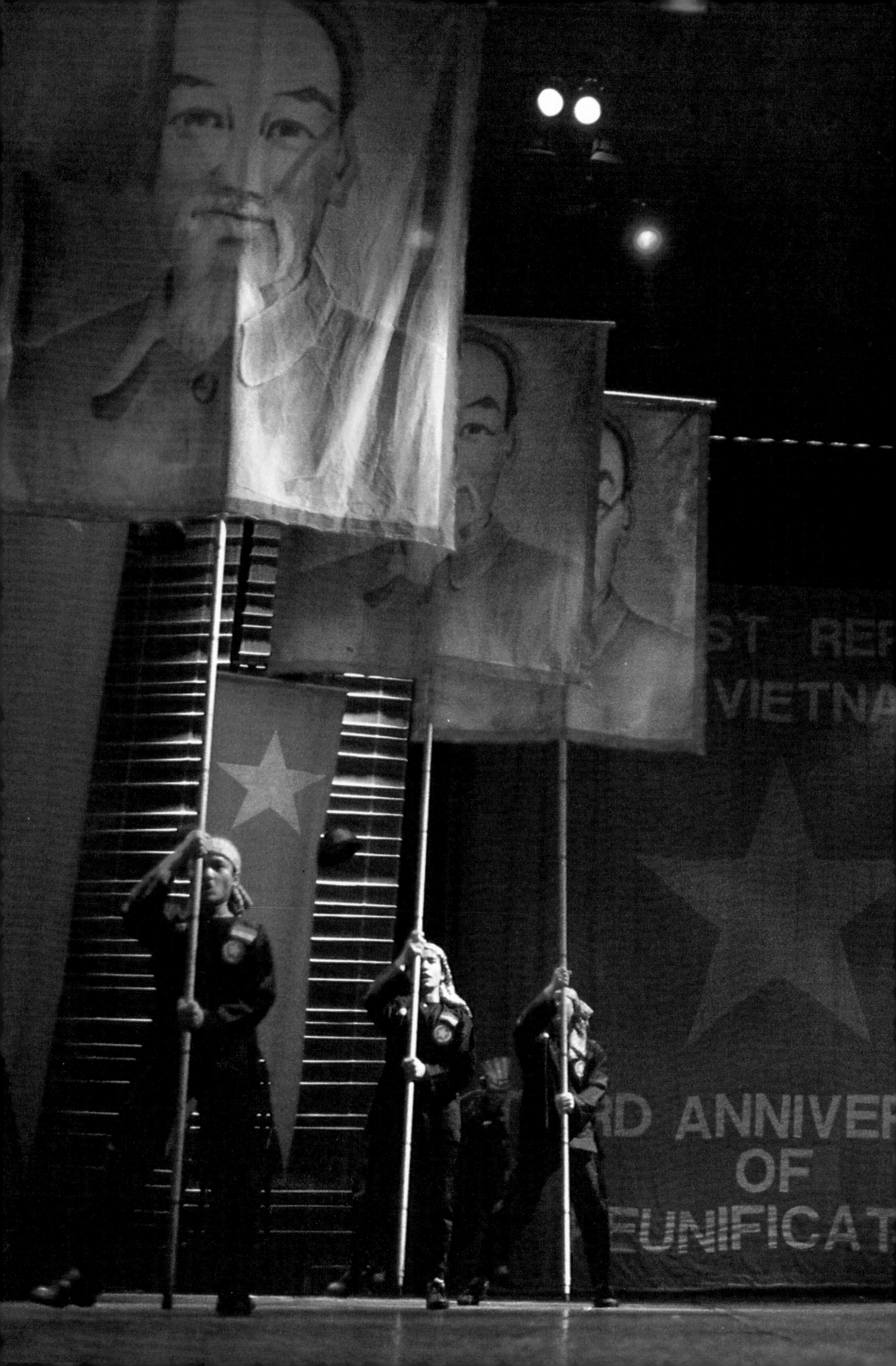
ST REP
VIETNA
RD ANNIVER
OF
EUNIFICAT

Above   'Three years of school was nice,
            In rice fields, planting rice'

Opposite   'Please let me hide in peace!'

Following page   'There is a secret
                     That you don't know'

Top   'Don't touch my son'

Bottom   'I have no other choice,
                What I must do I will'

Following spread   'This is the hour,
                This is our land'

Above   'Miss Saigon, in her crown,
        I made Queen of the town'

Opposite   'I hear the voice of my soldier
        Telling me to bring . . . his son'

Following spread   'No place, no home,
        No life, no hope'

Above   The Engineer, Kim and Tam join the boat-people

Opposite   'They're called *bui doi*,
    The dust of life'

Following pages   'I'm rounding up sheep
    To fleece here in Bangkok'

Opposite 'Girls! I got girls!'

Above 'You leave this to me,
Just play little mother'

Following page 'I'm here! I'm here! I'm never dead,
I'm here! I am the truth inside your head'

Top 'We'll get plenty of word when the VC attack'

Bottom 'The word is, we must be out by dawn'

Following pages 'I must get in there – listen, anyone!'

'Why in the world should I be saved
Instead of her?'

Previous spread 'There is no one to find here!
They have left us behind here!'

Above 'Then you must take Tam with you'

Opposite 'Kim was here –
The one who had to tell her was me'

Above   'In Bangkok, he will go
                To American schools'

Opposite   'What's that I smell in the air?
                    The American Dream'

Following spread   'Skyscrapers, neon and chrome,
                            The American Dream'

Opposite   'There I will crown,
                  Miss Chinatown'

Above   'Though I seem far away,
                I'll be watching you too'

Following spread   'How in one night have we come . . . so far?'

9 Traumas

While the words, and the music, were being pieced together, Mackintosh was busy assembling the production team for *Miss Saigon*. It was, tragically, to lead to the dismantling of the partnership that lay behind the success of *Les Misérables*, and to one of the major theatrical feuds of our time.

From the moment when Boublil and Schönberg first played Mackintosh their original French tape of Act One of *Miss Saigon*, their assumption was that Trevor Nunn, who had directed *Les Misérables*, would also direct the new show.

In the end, Trevor Nunn was not involved, and this was to result in an enduring break between him and Cameron Mackintosh. The rift was not simply the result of a personality clash, one of the inevitable ups and downs in the creation of *Miss Saigon*, or indeed any piece of theatre, but an exemplary illustration of how major misunderstandings can occur even among people who have worked together, and of the uncertainties of show business even for someone as famous as Trevor Nunn, one of the greatest living theatrical directors. It is a ruthless world of professed permanent friendships and loyalties and shifting interests. Musical theatre is affected more by such shifting patterns, for unlike the relatively simple world of movie-making, where certain stars, directors or scriptwriters are immediately 'bankable', in musical theatre the only star is the show itself. It is that which is remembered, and enters into legend, even if individuals (like the late Rex Harrison in *My Fair Lady*) achieve fame, and star status, in the process.

Inevitably, the producer becomes the all-powerful *Deus ex machina*, continually faced with difficult choices, for in musical theatre there is no such thing as a universal talent. A superb lyricist for one genre may turn out to be completely unsuitable for another and the same is true of performers. The producer's job is to use all his resources to make his endeavour as successful as possible. In the process, friendships, loyalties and personal ties must become irrelevant. The behind-the-scenes preparations of any piece of musical theatre are a mixture of cold-blooded planning, Machiavellian power-ploys and what, to some onlookers, looks very much like Borgian intrigues and blood-letting. None of the apparent cruelty is gratuitous: it's simply that, at any given time, the focus of the show may change, individuals become available as they juggle their own careers, and what looks like an obvious choice may turn out, in retrospect, to have been less than perfect. There is also, inevitably, the question of temperament and the mix of personalities involved. Producing a piece of musical theatre is not only more complicated than producing a movie, it is also much more of a team effort, and as such, the choice of partners is crucial. All those with relevant experience understand this and it's surprising how little bitterness there is. Directors, performers and stage designers all know that the producer's logic dictates what, occasionally, can be very harsh terms.

Trevor Nunn, however, a star in his own right, must have assumed that *Miss Saigon* was his to direct should he want to do so. He was unaware until much later that Cameron Mackintosh had private misgivings about his suitability for the show from the very beginning, and, in devoting considerable thought to the choice of the ideal director, realised that Nunn was, perhaps, *a* candidate rather than *the* candidate. 'Trevor Nunn is one of the world's great directors,' he says, 'and I respect him enormously. What happened was all my fault . . . My very first instinct was that [he] was, probably, not the perfect director for this particular piece,' Mackintosh recalls. 'I considered Michael Bennett, for the shifting musical rhythms of "Miss Saigon" would, I thought, appeal to him. Alas, he was too sick even to consider it. I approached Jerome Robbins, who toyed with the idea, but finally decided this was not quite his world. We left the question of the director in limbo, and then, early in 1987, Trevor Nunn asked me point-blank: "What's happening to 'Miss Saigon'? Am I not directing it?" I stalled, deliberately. My answer was that there was no director – yet. For me to be able to make up my mind, I said, there had to be a fully finished draft. The whole show, I implied, was very different from "Les Misérables", where Trevor Nunn's contribution had been essential, and indeed invaluable, during the actual writing process. "Miss Saigon" was an original creation, not, like "Les Mis", an adaptation.'

The subject was raised again a few months later, at the time of the Sydney opening of *Les Misérables* in November 1987. 'We had a long heart-to-heart talk,' Mackintosh recalls, 'and I expressed my reservations quite frankly. Nunn's international reputation had begun with his memorable years as artistic director at Stratford-on-Avon. Shakespeare apart, my feeling was that his greatest gift, as a director, was in taking classic themes, as in "Nicholas Nickleby" and "Les Misérables", and turning them into relevant, contemporary shows. I was having second thoughts about him because "Miss Saigon" was so very different – it *was* contemporary.'

Alain Boublil, who with Claude-Michel Schönberg also sat in on a dinner with Trevor Nunn, remembers only that Nunn had some strong reservations over the saxophone number, 'The Last Night Of The World', and that this somewhat alarmed him. But Trevor Nunn's involvement was neither terminated nor confirmed at this point. It was still up in the air, and indeed, as Mackintosh says, Trevor Nunn himself implied that in the absence of a firm offer he would soon be unable to take it on, for he was deluged with propositions. 'Of course you are,' Mackintosh remembers saying, 'you're one of the greatest directors in the world. I realise I will have to take my chances.'

The problem was compounded by the very considerable personal differences between Mackintosh and Nunn. Both have strong, egocentric personalities, and relations between them, during the making of *Les Misérables*, had never been easy. Nunn had fought tooth and nail the cuts that Mackintosh had sought to impose. Beyond this, the two men had realised early on that they would probably never become close friends. Both demand and, through charm and sheer force of personality, obtain the whole-hearted devotion of their teams, from whom they expect unwavering loyalty. They could both see that their relationship might breed conflict. There was also a difference in their lifestyles and interests, and they had very different circles of friends. 'I've known you for six or seven years and I don't know any more about you than I did seven years ago,' Mackintosh told Nunn as the 'Les Mis' première neared. 'I admire you more and know you less.'

Although Mackintosh still had no other obvious candidate in mind, he continued to harbour the nagging suspicion that, for all his extraordinary gifts, Trevor Nunn might not be the ideal person to direct *Miss Saigon*. With an American launch then planned, Mackintosh also felt that an American director might be an asset, which was why he had considered both Bennett and Robbins. Furthermore, as time went on, he realised that Trevor Nunn's energy and compulsive need to work were pushing him in several directions at once. A hyperactive workaholic, Nunn had no self-doubts concerning his ability to tackle several things at once, and felt that he even thrived on the sheer diversity of different shows in the making. There was *Chess*, which he had taken over from an already ailing Michael Bennett at the very last minute, and had turned into a huge success in London. He was engaged on a massive rewrite and adaptation of *Chess* for an American audience on Broadway, against the advice of his lyricist, Tim Rice, with whom he had parted company. And there was *Aspects of Love*, a longstanding Andrew Lloyd Webber project, which he confidently assumed he could direct in conjunction with *Miss Saigon*. Mackintosh felt that *Miss Saigon* was such a major undertaking that it precluded Trevor Nunn from directing *Aspects of Love*. Andrew Lloyd Webber felt the same about *his* planned production. Both *Miss Saigon* and *Aspects of Love*, scheduled to open in London during the same season in the same year (1989), had every chance of being reproduced around the world like *Cats* and *Les Misérables* and Mackintosh felt strongly that no single director could do justice to both of them, could physically find the time to supervise, and direct, two shows that might require his presence in different parts of the world at conflicting times. Mackintosh and Webber tacitly hoped that Nunn would choose one or the other. Trevor Nunn, of course, disagreed. He wanted to do both, and wrote a joint letter to the two producers saying so.

In his reply to Nunn, Mackintosh recalled that 'In Australia, I frankly, and in great depth, expressed to you why I wasn't willing to make an offer to you at the time, and indeed what my artistic reservations were about your suitability to direct the piece . . . I *never* said you could not direct "Aspects of Love". I only said that I was not prepared to have any director direct two musical productions of such international potential within the same year.'

At this stage, Andrew Lloyd Webber was having second thoughts about *Aspects of Love*. He was also, very discreetly, sounding out a young director called Nicholas Hytner as its possible director, should he go ahead with it after all. Mackintosh learnt of this, and decided that, with Nunn out of the running for *Aspects of Love*, he would after all be free to do *Miss Saigon*. Since he was still without an obvious alternative candidate he now decided that it would be foolish to turn his back on Nunn's experience and track record. He contacted Trevor Nunn's lawyer, Bill Fournier, and formal negotiations began.

Then Nunn started work on the new, 'American' version of *Chess*, and all of Mackintosh's fears and apprehensions returned. Specifically, Mackintosh was afraid that the *Chess* precedent would repeat itself and that Nunn would impose on *Miss Saigon* an imprint that might not be the one either he or the writing-composing team wanted. As one of the best-known theatrical directors in the world, Nunn assumed that he was to have total control over all areas of the production, including the lyrics. Mackintosh feared that such control would diminish his own producer's role, which he saw as realising the authors' creation in the form most acceptable to *them*. He also feared that what was happening to the American *Chess* production might seriously prejudice *Miss Saigon*'s chances of success, for it was well known in New York that, during the run-up to *Chess*, after the falling-out of Nunn and Tim Rice, the atmosphere on the set was tense, and that some members of Nunn's own production team felt he was pushing it in a direction which they, like Rice, felt was wrong, by 'over-Americanising' it. The possibility that Nunn might behave with Boublil and Schönberg as he had behaved with Rice, that he would deliver not their show, but his version of it, was, for Mackintosh, a nightmarish prospect. He knew that the French team's confidence had grown, and that they might respond differently to Nunn this time around.

Around the same time as Mackintosh was experiencing these fears, he saw a production of *Anything Goes*, directed by Jerry Zaks, and was immensely impressed. Reluctantly, but with the ruthlessness that is the hallmark of successful producers, Mackintosh told Bill Fournier that he wanted to terminate negotiations and that Trevor Nunn would not, after all, be directing *Miss Saigon*.

'I did so deliberately, *before* going to see "Chess",' says Mackintosh, 'because I knew that otherwise I would be accused of making up my mind on the basis of the "Chess" preview, which would have been unfair.'

It would of course be wrong to assume that the Broadway production of *Chess* had *no* bearing on Mackintosh's decision. He even asked both Boublil and Schönberg to make a trip to New York specially to take in an early preview performance. But the point Mackintosh adamantly makes is that his mind was made up *before* seeing it, and that its subsequent fate was irrelevant to his decision. In retrospect, it became clear to Mackintosh that he delayed far too long in acting on his apprehensions. 'I simply should have stuck to my very first instinctive feeling that Trevor Nunn was not the right person to direct "Miss Saigon",' Mackintosh says. 'Afterwards, I wrote a deeply apologetic letter to Nunn, taking the full blame for letting the situation get out of hand.'

These were harrowing times for Trevor Nunn. He knew, from the early responses of professionals and close friends, that *Chess* was too long, and had to be cut. He sensed that Mackintosh's reaction to a particularly unfortunate early preview performance had been unfavourable. Boublil and Schönberg were also worried by the preview they saw of *Chess*, but they were equally perturbed at the idea that someone unknown to them might be called in. 'It was a great upset for us,' Schönberg said later, 'because we always assumed that Nunn would direct it.' There were, he added, 'dark rumours to the effect that Trevor Nunn had hinted that the music was too derivative, that much of it would have to be rewritten, and this scared us.' What followed was a week of anguish all round.

At the suggestion of Bill Fournier, Mackintosh and Nunn finally met a few days before the *Chess* première, while the previews were still on. Nunn behaved as if he still assumed that he would direct, though his lawyer had already tentatively broken the bad news to him. Nunn was furious. As a mutual friend put it, 'It was not so much the firing itself as the timing that upset him.'

Mackintosh, once he realised that Nunn *had* been told that he would not direct *Miss Saigon*, but assumed otherwise, was angry, and contemptuous of what he regarded as an extremely devious power ploy. The two have not been on speaking terms since. Their falling-out was one of the major subjects of conversation in the London and New York theatre world, though it never made the headlines at the time.

Mackintosh's director was now Jerry Zaks, whose *Anything Goes* had been a tremendous New York hit, and he, together with Boublil, Schönberg and Maltby had already begun discussing the words and music of *Miss Saigon* when a problem of a completely different order arose: it became apparent there was no theatre on Broadway remotely suitable for *Miss Saigon*. *Phantom of the Opera*, *Les Misérables* and *Cats* were all playing to full houses. The Imperial, which had been considered for *Miss Saigon*, was no longer available, having been booked for the dance retrospective, *Jerome Robbins' Broadway*, and the Mark Hellinger Theatre, which Cameron Mackintosh was most set on, was already booked for the *Legs Diamond* musical.

Nicholas Hytner

Simultaneously, for such are the vagaries of show business, two major London theatres became unexpectedly available: the Prince Edward (because of the ending of the London production of *Chess*) and the Theatre Royal, Drury Lane, once David Merrick had decided to close *42nd Street* which had been running there. There were now compelling reasons to switch the venue to London: the Theatre Royal, with 2,300 seats, is London's largest, most prestigious theatre. It was, for Mackintosh, a significant venue, for it was here that his career in the theatre had begun, as cleaner and stagehand, at the age of eighteen, back in 1965. This in turn posed an insuperable problem for Zaks: for family reasons, he felt unable to spend a year or more in London. At the same time, Nicholas Hytner, the British director Andrew Lloyd Webber had had in mind as a possible director for *Aspects of Love*, had ended his flirtation with Webber's Really Useful Group. Trevor Nunn was now officially assigned to direct *Aspects of Love* and Hytner was now available – or would be, after completing his direction of *Ghetto* for the National Theatre.

Mackintosh anxiously awaited Hytner's opinion on a production team that had been on stand-by for months, if not years. Once hired, the director's word is law, so it was with considerable relief that he learnt that Hytner accepted without reservations the team already assembled. One of its key members was Bob Avian, Michael Bennett's long-time friend and partner who had worked with Mackintosh choreographing *Follies* in 1986. Avian is not only one of America's outstanding choreographers, but he did himself tour Vietnam in the Sixties with a bus-truck-and-helicopter version of *Hello, Dolly!* He therefore had a highly personal interest in the theme. It was Avian who told Mackintosh that 'musical design is either based in architecture or painted scenery – and this one is architecture.' John Napier was a designer and theatrical architect *par excellence*, and, as Mackintosh recalls, 'I didn't need to think any more.' Napier's long-time collaborators, lighting designer David Hersey, and Andreane Neofitou, who had designed the costumes for *Les Misérables* and *Cats*, were also natural choices. Andrew Bruce, the accoustics specialist, had a special relationship with Alain Boublil and Claude-Michel Schönberg that predated even Mackintosh's *Les Misérables* production, for he it was who had designed the concealed VHF microphones used in the original French-language version of *Les Misérables* at Paris's Palais des Sports in 1980.

With the entire production team in place, preparations were almost complete. Casting, at this stage, was still a long way off. This was a challenge: a quarter of the performers had to look like authentic Vietnamese – and they had to be able to sing a complicated, demanding score.

Constructing the set inside the Theatre Royal

10 Problems Resolved

Looking back on those first, crisis-ridden months, Boublil and Schönberg recognise that the serious business of getting *Miss Saigon* ready for the stage really began with the arrival on the scene of Nicholas Hytner, who, though at the time (1988) relatively unknown to the general public, had a string of critical successes to his credit in opera and straight theatre.

In many respects, the backgrounds of Hytner and Nunn were similar: both had made their mark as directors while still undergraduates at Cambridge, and both had risen through repertory and provincial companies, attracting the attention of major producers along the way. Thirty-two, Hytner had already had an unusually varied career. At eighteen, having just left Manchester Grammar School, and before going up to Cambridge, he directed the amateur but highly regarded Manchester-based Wilmslowe opera group in a production of *Così fan tutte*. At the Cambridge ADC (Amateur Dramatic Club) he directed *Love's Labour's Lost* and productions of the Brecht-Weill *Threepenny Opera* and *The Rise and Fall of the City of Mahagonny*, with an all-student company including an orchestra totalling over a hundred people. Active in Footlights, the exclusive satiric revue company, he attended the 'fringe' Edinburgh Festival and immediately afterwards started working as an assistant director, first in Glasgow, then with the English National and Kent Opera Companies and at the Coliseum before breaking out as a fully-fledged director at the Kent Opera. He came to Cameron Mackintosh's attention in 1985 with a stage version at the Chichester Theatre of *The Scarlet Pimpernel*, an Edwardian melodrama based on Baroness Orczy's famous novel.

So taken was Mackintosh with this production, which included a few songs and elaborate 'numbers', some of them deliberately camp, satirising the very genre of historical melodramas, that he thought of Hytner as a possible director for Stephen Sondheim's *Follies*, which he was producing in London. Sondheim went to see *Pimpernel*, was baffled by its quintessentially English humour, and Hytner did not direct *Follies*. Instead, he spent the following two years in Manchester, working uninterruptedly on a wide range of productions from Schiller's *Don Carlos* to *The Country Wife*. His production of *Xerxes* caused the Paris Opera director to invite him to be guest director there for Handel's *Julius Caesar*, an opera seldom performed. Assignments in Amsterdam, Houston and Geneva followed.

With Trevor Nunn temporarily out of the running to direct

Aspects of Love, Andrew Lloyd Webber approached Hytner. The dates, however, kept changing, and clashed with the National Theatre production of *Ghetto* he was also scheduled to direct. So, when Mackintosh finally phoned him, 'coming absolutely clean', as Hytner recalls, he explained how he came to be the third director involved in *Miss Saigon*.

For all his slight build and self-deprecatory manner (when I first saw him I was irresistibly reminded of a youthful Alec Guinness), Hytner is someone who knows his own mind, and says what he thinks in a forthright, sometimes brutal way. It was some time before Boublil and Schönberg, somewhat traumatised by the arrival and departure of two directors, were fully at ease with this determined young man, though they soon became firm friends. Hytner highlighted the very areas of the show about which they themselves felt somewhat hesitant. 'In "Miss Saigon", the important thing to bear in mind was the dramatic structure, and it's simply not possible to know exactly and immediately what needs to be done,' Hytner says. 'I could tell that certain things were too discursive, that some things had to be simplified. The Suzuki character, Mia, turned out to be unnecessary, so she went.'

In rehearsal

Most of the problems, he recalls, were in Act Two. With Hytner's arrival, some sequences were changed, and the narrative structure (Chris and Ellen's journey to Bangkok, the confrontation between Kim and Ellen) altered both to turn Ellen into a three-dimensional character and to explore the interrelation of characters in more depth. Some of the changes occurred just three weeks before previews began. I remember sitting in on a dinner in a private dining-room at the Groucho Club attended only by the 'hard core' production team. Mackintosh, Hytner, Boublil, Schönberg and Maltby examined Act Two with a surprisingly dispassionate critical gaze. That weekend, Schönberg wrote two new songs and the whole hotel-room scene was changed. No harsh words were spoken, no egos were on display. Boublil and Schönberg, Hytner recalls, 'buckled down like good little soldiers. They knew that everything that had been said was based on total respect for their work. The difference between a big popular musical, which is what "Miss Saigon" is, and the sort of play I might do in the subsidised theatre is that this has to work every inch of the way.'

It takes anything up to six months to prepare the sets for something as complicated as *Miss Saigon* and long before casting or rehearsals began John Napier, the prize-winning set designer of *Les Misérables*, was hard at work. 'I had been fascinated by the Vietnam War and had read a good deal about it, but the plight of the *bui doi* came as something new to me,' Napier says. 'It was a far cry, in almost all ways, from "Les Mis".'

John Napier

'"Les Misérables",' Napier recalls, 'left a lot to the imagination. Here was a script with much more specific stage directions, much less poetic licence. From the stage designer's point of view, it was much more demanding, not only because it was more filmic in its presentation, but also dealt with events that had been made familiar all over the world thanks to TV coverage. It had the sweep of an epic, but was also of an intimate nature at times, dealing with two, or at most three people. You can never compete with movies, because you can only put the essence of each scene on stage, and the question you always ask yourself is: to what degree do you go to make it believable? Getting the balance right between stylisation and naturalism is the name of the game. It means using, at times, devices that are very painterly, diaphanous and gauze-like yet with hard-edge images on them.'

In *Les Misérables*, Napier's fundamental device had been to use a 'revolve', a moving stage, to give everything a cinematic effect. This, clearly, would not do for *Miss Saigon*. Instead, Napier decided, in order to 'tell the story in a fluid sequence of events which is the theatre designer's art', to use a well-known device, 'trucks', or moving platforms, as a means of 'delivering objects to the centre of the stage'. The sheer size of London's Drury Lane Theatre almost compelled him to do this: to bring a room, a bed into focus, to centre stage, the entire unit had to slide forward on concealed rails – operated by small computer-driven engines. Ironically, *Miss Saigon*'s most dramatic scene, on stage – the nightmare sequence in which Kim relives her experience in front of the US Embassy, with the 'Huey' helicopter landing on the roof and taking off with the last handful of Marines, including her lover, Chris – posed the fewest problems.

The helicopter is secured to a concealed lift, with a counterbalance, on an articulated hinge-pulley at the back of the stage, and – when not in use – is out of sight, high up near the roof. It is suspended from a couple of huge cables on a gimbal enabling it to rotate in any direction, and the whole thing is manually operated by remote-control joysticks. This, plus the realistic noise, gives it its incredible authenticity. The blades are, in fact, thin cords, with centrifugal force providing the illusion of a heavy, whirling blade motion. The whole thing is a triumph of illusion, based on relatively simple mechanics. Long before Hytner was chosen as director, in April 1989, the helicopter model had been approved by Mackintosh, and was being built by a specialist firm in Norfolk to specifications drawn up by the legendary Mike Barnett, the same engineer who had designed the mobile barricades for *Les Misérables*.

'It's really very straightforward,' said Napier. 'Early on we intended to blow bits of debris into the audience to simulate the kind of dust storm that landing helicopters provoke, but we feared some of it might get lodged in the musical instruments in the orchestra pit. Finally, we did without because the overall effect was staggering enough without the debris, the people on the stage giving it its proper scale. Nothing is gratuitous, or "special effects" only; I hate that. Everything happens with a purpose, because the story requires it.'

Even for a veteran like Napier, the first test run of the helicopter at the Drury Lane Theatre was a thrill. 'It's only when you see it on the stage that you know whether it's going to work or not.'

The theatre's sheer size – for the Drury Lane is not only the biggest commercial theatre in Europe, but also has the most space backstage – was both an advantage and a drawback. The Ho Chi Minh statues (driven by hydraulic rams) had to be scaled down for the Broadway Theatre stage. So did the Cadillac in the Act Two 'American Dream' sequence. This, in the original London version, was a real Cadillac, bought for $6,000 from a car collector while it was still being shipped from the US to Britain. 'The Cadillac was something I had suggested very early on, and was told: forget it,' Napier recalls. 'Then, three weeks before the previews started, they said: remember that Cadillac idea you had? So we started scouring the country for one – and couldn't find any. We bought the one we used on the basis of a photograph the owner showed us, while it was still somewhere in mid-Atlantic, aboard a cargo ship. We then scooped everything out, but it's still quite heavy. For the Broadway theatre, we have had to build a scaled-down model.'

Long before casting began, Napier had built a stage set model, complete with 'trucks' and rails, and when Hytner was hired to direct they would spend one day a week playing with the model, working out stage and prop requirements with a script which, like all musical theatre scripts, was subject to change. Napier had no time to go either to Ho Chi Minh City or to Bangkok, relying instead on photographs of the war (especially Philip Jones Griffiths's remarkable book *Vietnam Inc.*), and on descriptions I was able to provide. The sets had to be designed not only for wear and tear but for long usage. 'When Cameron Mackintosh produces a show, longevity matters,' says Napier. 'Everything has to be built to last from five to ten years.'

Helicopter test-run

11 Storytelling Beats

Despite the convenient shorthand of 'the new British musical' by the '"Les Mis" team', there were some striking and revealing differences between the makers of *Miss Saigon* and those of its predecessor. In 1985, Cameron Mackintosh was still seen by the Broadway establishment as an offshore eccentric. Four years later, the maverick had become the mainstream. Richard Maltby, New York through and through, was the first of the *ancien régime* to throw in his lot with the revolutionaries, and others soon followed. 'The text by Alain has me,' he said, 'the music by Claude-Michel has an American orchestrator, Bill Brohn, and the staging by a brilliant English director, Nick Hytner, has an American choreographer, Bob Avian. I don't think it's calculated, but there is some kind of support system at work.

'The reason I'm here is simple,' continued Maltby. 'In England at this moment there is a group of people who are rediscovering the form and pushing it in a direction that is risky and dangerous. That's what all the great musicals did in New York in the Forties and Fifties.' Because of Andrew Lloyd Webber's success, too many of the recent developments in musical theatre are presented in crude "Brits versus Broadway" headlines. It's probably truer to say, though, that Cameron Mackintosh is *internationalising* the musical, looking for his collaborators beyond the West End to Europe, North America, the Philippines even, until the right people for each show are all in place. The result is that the passports of his creative team are almost as varied as the productions' eventual destinations.

None the less, the presence of Bob Avian on the team was the clearest indication of how Mackintosh was now in a position to call upon the services of Broadway's best. Avian is a walking (or maybe step-kicking) history of modern American show dance: after playing on Broadway in *West Side Story* and *Hello, Dolly!*, he worked with Michael Bennett as associate choreographer, assistant director and/or producer on such shows as *Promises, Promises, Company, A Chorus Line* and *Dreamgirls*; his list of collaborators includes such Main Stem giants as Neil Simon, Alan Jay Lerner, Hal Prince and Stephen Sondheim. An easy-going man content to rest on his laurels – or, at any rate, his converted hunting lodge in north-west Connecticut – Avian turns down most of the projects he's offered, reluctant to commit himself to months of work in claustrophobic downtown rehearsal rooms. So why say yes to Mackintosh?

'Well, when Cameron calls you, you know the show is going to happen,' he says. 'That's not true of many producers these days.' Even so, it was with some reluctance that Avian agreed to choreograph Mackintosh's 1987 London production of *Follies*, a show he'd helped stage in its original Broadway incarnation. 'All during "Follies", Cameron was trying to turn me on to "Miss Saigon", playing me songs in French which I couldn't understand. I told him, "Let's just go one show at a time. You may end up hating me."' Like Richard Maltby and Bill Brohn before him, though, Avian found himself playing Schönberg's demo tape over and over, and slowly falling in love with the emotional sweep of the music. Without reading the script, he said yes.

When he *did* read the script, he got quite a shock. *Follies* is a choreographer's show, a succession of splashy pastiche numbers, populated by leggy girls in fabulous costumes. But what could *Miss Saigon* offer? 'When I read it, I realised, "God, there's so little musical staging." There was much less than I eventually got, but at that time I didn't see anything.' Mackintosh, though, knew what he was doing: 'My first reaction on hearing Act One of "Miss Saigon" was that ten years ago I would have gone straight to Michael Bennett and Bob Avian and asked them – because of the darkness. I could see Michael weaving a black tapestry through the whole thing.' But by that time Bennett was dying, and for Avian this would be the first time in over twenty years that he'd worked on a brand new musical without his old partner. 'I knew Bob could do it. He isn't merely a choreographer,' Mackintosh points out. 'He directs through movement.'

Bob Avian

Avian, however, found the black tapestry a little daunting. Even 'The Morning Of The Dragon' and 'The American Dream' didn't strike him as particularly promising. 'My choreographer friends asked me what the big opportunities were and I told them: the reunification of fucking Vietnam and an attack on American materialism. I read it and I go, "Wait a minute! Where are the showgirls? Where are the tap numbers?"'

Avian is indulging in a little self-mockery, playing up to the popular misconception of choreographers – that they're the guys you wheel on when you need a kickline or a buck'n'wing or Gwen Verdon doing 'If My Friends Could See Me Now'; and if you don't have dances, you don't need a choreographer. 'When you think of "My Fair Lady",' Avian says, 'you never think about the dancing. But there's a lot of movement in the show. The "Ascot Gavotte", for example, is one of the best staged sequences ever. That's "dance", too, I think. So I'm not necessarily turned on to a lot of dance steps, I'm turned on to an idea. Having a lot of steps may get you a Tony Award, but it won't always make a good show.'

After discussing his billing with Mackintosh, Avian opted for the credit 'Musical Staging by . . . ' rather than 'Choreography'. It doesn't make much difference in practice, but it lets anybody who studies the poster know that, unlike *Follies*, this is not a dance musical; there are staged numbers, but don't expect tap-shoes and spangled tights. In the days before he graduated to the hyphenated superstager status of 'choreographer-director', Michael Bennett used to complain that very few people – whether audience, critics or practitioners – really knew what a choreographer did. 'It can', said Avian, 'be a ballad where they're standing still for the entire number. On "Losing My Mind" in "Follies", I said to Julia Mackenzie, "You're going to raise this arm on this line, that arm on that line, and you're gonna raise 'em both together on "You said you *loved me*!" And she said, "Oh, good. Thank you."' Avian shrugged. 'That's musical staging.'

In a show like *Miss Saigon*, what Avian calls 'arm choreography' is often more important than fancy footwork. With the amplified sound system now used in musicals, it's sometimes hard in the crowd scenes to tell who's speaking. In Act Two, Kim relives the fall of Saigon, as the scene dissolves to a nightmare sequence outside the US Embassy, a sea of Vietnamese scrambling at the wire fences: 'Take me with you! Take my children!' begs one, 'I helped the CIA,' cries another. To help identify these anonymous refugees, Avian gave them what he describes as 'rose-bloom' moments, so that on their vocal lines each character would stretch out his arm and reach further up the gates. That way, at least you would have some sense of them as individuals: they were, in effect, 'close-ups' within the broad panorama, helping you to focus on particular lines.

To Avian, this is the essence of dramatic choreography – not dance steps, but 'storytelling beats' which tell the audience where to look. 'One afternoon, I was playing around in rehearsal', he said, 'and I came up with one little moment for the nightmare sequence. Chris is saying "Please be home" and Kim is down right going "I am lost here", and I have this girl fainting in slow motion while the whole group goes on behind her. Even though they weren't choreographer's numbers, I added little moments like that here and there.'

Most of *Miss Saigon* is staged very naturalistically, but, to make the numbers move, Avian implanted a few emphases, as on 'Tonight I will be Miss Saigon'. 'When you hit that line,' he told the girls, 'hit a diagonal. Make sure your head goes up and you look at that light . . . ' It's a dreamy stylised touch which then slides seamlessly back into the grittier, more earthbound staging of the overall number. And, because Kim is the only girl whose head isn't at an angle, who's looking straight out at us, we're drawn subliminally to her from the beginning of the show.

Avian had experienced clubs like the Engineer's at first hand. In the Sixties, he went with Mary Martin and the *Hello Dolly* company to Vietnam to entertain the troops. 'They'd fly us out in the morning to where we were playing, and we'd get back to our hotel, which had barbed wire all around it and soldiers outside the window, and they'd say, "Never go downtown alone." So I'd go with this friend of mine, and it was frightening just to see this guy hunched in a corner, in the shadows, outside some closed-up store front, and he knows you're American. It's a tone you're left with: heat, humidity, discomfort, danger, just lurking.'

Company work-out

Avian's familiarity with the milieu and his extensive Broadway résumé make you wonder why, unlike Bennett, Bob Fosse, Jerome Robbins and others, he's never wanted to move on to directing. A mellow modest man, he sees himself as a good collaborator, happy to serve another man's vision of the show. In a typically quirky move by Mackintosh, though, Avian was approached as choreographer before a director had been settled on, an inversion of the usual practice. So over the next few months, he found himself adapting his ideas to whichever director hoved into view. He liked Trevor Nunn but believes 'he has never had what I would call a successful relationship with a choreographer. Perhaps that's why the English choreographer hasn't happened yet. It has with the writers, with Andrew Lloyd Webber and Claude-Michel and Alain; it has with directors like Trevor and Mike Ockrent; but not with choreographers.'

Avian sees the Boublil–Schönberg and Lloyd Webber shows as operas – essentially vocal pieces, where you're lucky if you can squeeze any movement in. Unfortunately, what movement there is often does look *squeezed* in: in, say, *Aspects of Love* or *Chess*, it was very obvious where Nunn broke off and his choreographer was briefly allowed to take over. To be fair, that tension between director and choreographer is something that dates back over half a century, to George Abbott and George Balanchine. Choreographers are often looking to land routines of their own, regardless of the show, while directors can grow to resent the way the most memorable pieces of staging in a musical belong to somebody else. In a successful collaboration it should be impossible to spot the join, to see where the director hands over to the choreographer.

With Jerry Zaks on board, Avian got down to talking about specifics. 'Suppose we have really *mean* North Vietnamese soldiers, and they're doing, like, these modern ballets where they're jumping and turning and hitting the peasants with the butts of their rifles . . .'

'Well, er, I don't know about that,' said Zaks, cautiously. War is not naturally balletic, and to have abandoned 'reality' so recklessly would have been an invitation to ridicule. To many people, the most dated element of Forties and Fifties musicals are those self-consciously arty dream ballets. As Hal Prince once said, 'The old musicals used to dance in depth, and it was embarrassing as hell – rolling around in torment.'

With Nicholas Hytner on the team, the show's staging language was finally settled. The Engineer, a lurid up-front character in both his manner and dress, had a larger-than-life extravagance to his numbers, but the love story had to be kept realistic. 'Kim and Chris are so direct,' Avian reckons, 'there's nothing theatrical about them. You'd lose a little bit of heart if you were suddenly to give them an erotic love ballet. If you were going to do it, you'd have to start from the moment you saw them – like when Tony and Maria meet in "West Side Story". There's a rule in musical theatre. During your first five minutes, you establish your vocabulary, your language for the piece. Anything you do in that first scene, you can do all evening long. But, if you start doing it in Scene Six, you're in big trouble.' For that reason, a lighter Fred-and-Ginger staging of 'The Last Night Of The World' had to be abandoned. Chris and Kim could never plausibly have moved with such gossamer grace and style. Instead, they cling together with a touching but clumsy urgency.

Hytner and Avian are an odd partnership by any standards: a director with a distinguished reputation in high art, a choreographer with a formidable appetite for what he himself describes as 'schlock' – action movies and daytime soap operas. Unfamiliar with his new collaborator's work, Avian arranged tickets to see Hytner's production of *Measure for Measure* at the Royal Shakespeare Company. An hour before curtain-up, he got cold feet: 'It's Saturday night. Do I really want to see "Measure for Measure"? Or would I rather go to "Die Hard"?' It was no contest: Avian settled for a Saturday night at the movies with Bruce Willis in *Die Hard*, and left Shakespeare for another day.

'Most nights, *I'd* prefer to see "Die Hard" rather than "Measure for Measure",' rationalised Hytner. 'Well, *some* nights . . . I have colleagues who aren't interested in popular culture, but I've always been. It doesn't call into question my devotion to high art as well.' Hytner resists the notion that, after opera and the classics, a big new musical was a departure for him. 'The rules of the American musical are not so very different from Aristotle's on how to write a play: where to punch, where to pull back, how to land. The eleven o'clock number [a Broadway expression referring to a powerful song introduced late in the second act, such as the title numbers of *Oklahoma!* and *Cabaret*] is a concept which would have been just as familiar to Sophocles under a different name. It's all showbiz,' he concluded, 'although I have to say that in the end

"King Lear" is perhaps better than "Miss Saigon".' 'Yes, but our dance routines are better,' retorted Mackintosh.

Once on board, Hytner went round to see the designer John Napier, who immediately junked the set he'd developed with Jerry Zaks. 'It was glossy, glitzy and brutal,' says Hytner, 'and I saw the show as more poetic, diaphanous, impressionistic. The only thing that stayed was the helicopter. Basically, he said, "Do you want to direct a musical with a helicopter in it?" I said, "Okay, fine."'

Any show which includes a helicopter must by definition be lavish. Yet in many respects the design for the show is quite spare. 'I always knew how I was going to do the nightmare sequence,' Hytner says, 'and it's the one scene where there's basically just a couple of walls and a fence. A lot of the piece is directed in a quasi-naturalistic operatic fashion, but the most interesting bits to me are the ones which pull away from that towards more of a "musical comedy" aesthetic (that's not exactly the right term, but it's the best I can do). I'd quite like to see how much further it can go in that direction.' Once Hytner had decided on his staging, Avian would add his own touches, tightening and fine-tuning the scene: as a result, *Miss Saigon* is a far more detailed work than many plays and musicals turn out.

Bob Avian demonstrating 'arm choreography'

Perhaps the clearest example of what staging can add to a text comes at the end of 'The Last Night Of The World'. In earlier drafts, the song had ended and Chris had then given Kim his gun: 'Take this. I'm taking you out with me. I'll arrange everything and come back for you.' The scene then moved into the next song, 'The Morning Of The Dragon', and a Vietcong teacher 're-educating' among others Gigi, Mimi and the Engineer. When the sequence finally took stage, though, Chris's dialogue – a prosaic 'book' exchange – had gone. Instead, the song stood by itself:

> A song
> Played on a solo saxophone –
> So stay with me
> And hold me tight
> And dance
> Like it's the last night
> > Of the world . . .

The lyrics are the devalued sentiments of a hundred catchpenny ballads, but for Kim and Chris they've come true: they really do love each other. In Hytner's staging, though, the last line is also made explicitly literal. The two have been, as Maltby says, 'dancing on the edge of the volcano', and as they finish singing, the music builds and builds and suddenly it *is* the last night of the world –

the fall of Saigon, April 1975. One insignificant love affair is swallowed up, as Chris and Kim's seedy rented room is pulled back and steel blinds snap shut, burying the old city for ever; one insinuating dance tune is guillotined by the brutish martial tempo heralding 'The Morning Of The Dragon' and the red banners and yellow stars of the Vietcong.

What's most remarkable about the scene is that, from the Drury Lane auditorium, Chris and Kim – two tiny figures on that huge stage – seem to be in close-up, a giant head shot almost. Then, before we know what's happening, we're suddenly aware of how small they are against that vast empty background – as if, in some personal movie in our minds, the camera has pulled back until they're tiny specks on the horizon. It's typical of a production which has the fluidity of film. 'I didn't want it to look like "Kismet" or "The King and I",' said Mackintosh. 'It couldn't have that sort of traditional scenery or any sense of "showbiz". And, as it all started to mesh, the lighting and design gave it a filmic quality. When you look at the clips of the show, you do actually think you're looking at a film.'

If only because of the challenge it represented, 'The Morning Of The Dragon' is Bob Avian's favourite number in the show. He had not been involved in the casting of the ensemble, where singing and Asian authenticity had to be the primary considerations. So he was forced to make the best of what were mostly non-dancing performers. 'I couldn't give them anything technical beyond their reach, so I asked them, "Can anybody pole-vault?" No one could, so I asked, "Does anybody here do acrobatics?" A tenor went, "I'm an acrobat." Well, that was a start. And most of them could discotheque, so I built on that. But it was still incredibly difficult getting them to understand "The Morning Of The Dragon". They had to sing very complicated harmonies and rhythm patterns: a five/four bar, then a four/four bar, then a five/four bar. That's already asking a lot, so to try and make them move as well . . . '
Because of the lyric, Hytner saw the number as 'street theatre':

Keith Burns (Thuy) and members of the company

> The morning of the dragon
> Truth lit up the street.
> The tiger we were stalking
> Walked on paper feet . . .

Avian agreed, and then asked: 'Can there be ribbons?' With such difficult music, he realised he couldn't give them any complicated steps. But anyone can wave ribbons, and that was all it took to give the number a sense of movement. In the best Broadway tradition, Avian had used the limitations of his resources to create a piece of memorable staging.

138

Having grappled with operas which are as unreal as you can get and so convention-loaded that a platoon of Avian's all-dancing Vietcong would pass unnoticed, Nick Hytner seemed determined to be as rigorous on the libretto as he could. 'It's at its best,' he said, 'when it's being hard, sassy, American. The phone conversations, the GI talk: that's all good, but some of the simple romantic lyrics are still disappointing. You sometimes think, "Did Hammerstein have the monopoly on all that?" Luckily, that's where Claude-Michel is at his strongest – and "Sun And Moon" is a good lyric.'

His main concern was with the character of Kim, whose language was steeped in Oriental mysticism. 'Nick just didn't want that,' says Richard Maltby. 'He wanted a very tough, realistic non-romantic romance. And we agreed with that. We didn't want "The World of Suzi Wong", with the little virgin or the prostitute with the heart of gold. And to have a girl who was talking to the gods drove Nick crazy. It was way over the top and smacked of operatic convention.'

'The Morning Of The Dragon' in rehearsal

'I felt all that "great sacred bird" stuff was a rather shallow Western idea of the way the Eastern mind works,' explains Hytner. 'It just rang false to me. And one of the reasons I didn't believe it is because I don't believe *they* did.'

Alain Boublil denied this and mounted a strong defence: 'I had to prove to him that there are many novels about girls the same age as Kim – twenty – whose life is shared between the modern world (they wear blue jeans like everyone else) and the cult of the ancestors – that respect for older values which sticks in their minds and will stick in their daughters' minds and their daughters' daughters'. What I probably exaggerated at the beginning was that mystical language, because it's helpful to be able to write in a more poetic way. But little by little, keeping the sun and moon images (which are crucial) but getting rid of the other things, she became more of a girl of today.'

'The initial discussion', says Hytner, 'is, "Are we saying the right things?" – which is easy. But, when you get down to "This line is no good", that's more difficult. I don't believe I ever tried to manipulate this piece into saying something different from what it wanted to say. But I did work very hard at making it say *better* what it wanted to say in the first place. Much of a director's job simply consists of saying to the writers: write this better.'

There were some casualties along the way, including Kim's pretty Act Two solo, 'Too Much For One Heart':

> Outside there is a war
> But here the night is still,
> The jasmine buds have bloomed

The way that jasmine will
And I have given birth
To a speckle of dust,
To a sparkle of light,
To a small hint of life:
Frail as a flower in the morning
Is this tiny work of art.
When I see his face before me,
This is too much for one heart . . .

'It was probably the most beautiful song in the show,' said Boublil sadly, 'but as a *song*. It proved to be useless in that form, and, according to Nick, it was holding up the show. So we rewrote it one night and it became a duet.' In its new form, the song covers Kim's meeting in Bangkok with Chris's friend John.

Hytner's strict, disciplined approach never brought him to blows with the authors – partly, he thinks, because everyone was so straightforward. 'When you say to Claude-Michel, "This is not good," he has a variety of responses, ranging from, "Yezz, you aire right, I just deed zees to make noise," to "No, I am vairy proud of this." And, when it's the latter, you think that's fine because he's being so candid. He and Alain are two big soppy sloppy sentimental Frenchmen. They wear their hearts on their sleeves, they're moved very easily, they're randy, they like movies, they like food. That's what they do, and what they do is *true*.'

What Hytner missed, however, perhaps because he's laboured so long in the withered vineyards of opera, is what he calls 'the particular excitement of the American musical': the fusion of dialogue, lyrics and music. He accepted that Boublil and Schönberg had written a through-composed work, but for a while he tried to persuade them to change. 'I'll try "Carmen" on them,' he thought. In its original form, Bizet's opera had no recitative, but instead short passages of dialogue very delicately underscored. 'It's sensational,' he says. 'Those are some of the most effective passages of opera ever written – with echoes or pre-echoes of all the great numbers in the score. Anyway, I tried it out on them: "Why can't we replace some of this recitative with underscoring and talk?"'

Boublil and Schönberg went away, mulled it over and then told the director: 'We can't do this.' Hytner accepted their decision: 'I didn't write it, *they* did. And in the end they should just say to me, "Fuck off and do what we wrote."'

12 Casting

On 15 October 1988, ten nervous Asians auditioned in London for parts in *Miss Saigon* before Boublil, Schönberg, Hytner and Mackintosh. Fifteen showed up on the second day. The six remaining candidates were outnumbered by press photographers by three to one on the third, and last, day. None was remotely suitable.

They had responded to an ad in the *Stage*, and before casting was complete Mackintosh's business manager, Nick Allott, and his team would go to extraordinary lengths to seek out talented Asian singers in unlikely places. Notices were posted up in Chinese restaurants in Soho, and in a large Buddhist temple in Wimbledon; ads were taken out in Vietnamese-language magazines in Paris and the word spread throughout Vietnamese associations in London and Paris. Every London-based South-East Asian embassy was also contacted. 'The staffs were co-operative but bemused,' Allott recalls. An official from the Vietnamese Embassy in London (which was to afford the company considerable assistance in the areas of both decor and costumes) politely pointed out that the title of the show was wrong: 'I think you mean Miss Ho Chi Minh city, Sir,' he told Allott.

Boublil, Schönberg and Hytner were determined to have as many real-life Asians in the cast as possible; *Madame Butterfly*-type make-up, though suitable enough for opera, would, they knew, be inadequate, especially for female members of the cast. Also, the physical demands made on performers in *Miss Saigon* required an authentic Asian litheness and grace.

Mackintosh had additional reasons to search far and wide in Britain for members of the cast. Equity, the British actors' union, vigilantly protects the interests of its members. As many company members as possible, he knew, would have to be recruited locally. The trouble was that, for all the size of the Asian community in Britain, singing candidates were in desperately short supply. All foreign 'imports' would have to be approved by Equity's powerful board.

The problem was compounded by an apparent shortage of singing Asians elsewhere. In New York, Vincent Liff, of Johnson-Liff Casting Associates, a major agency, reported back to Mackintosh that the search would be more difficult than anticipated. Allott circulated the cast breakdown to 300 British agents, and applications started pouring in by the sackful. Many former and current *Les Misérables* cast members also auditioned for the non-Asian parts.

The company was drawn from the Philippines, Holland, France, the USA, Italy, Hong Kong and Japan

141

In November 1988, Boublil, Schönberg, Hytner, Mackintosh and Liff set out on a whirlwind tour of the US and the Philippines. I accompanied them. The principal object of the trip was to find Miss Saigon, for the feeling was that once the title role had been cast, everything else would fall into place. Auditions began in New York, continued in Los Angeles and Hawaii and ended in Manila. Not for the first time, I noted in Mackintosh a cool gambler's detachment. As the only non-showbiz person in the group, I also marvelled at the calm optimism of all concerned, with rehearsals due to begin within three months and not a single part filled. I recalled, however, that during the *Les Misérables* casting, there had been no Jean Valjean until a few weeks before rehearsals started and that Patti LuPone had taken on the role of Fantine only *after* rehearsals had been in progress for a couple of weeks.

Chinese-Americans, Japanese-Americans, Filipino-Americans and a handful of genuine Vietnamese succeeded each other in a converted dance studio on Broadway on the first day. Hytner behaved throughout with exaggerated courtesy, never once interrupting, invariably thanking the performers profusely. 'Thank you *very* much, well done,' was a sign to me that he was crossing the candidate off his books. Very occasionally, he would question the candidate about her acting experience. Proof of real interest only came if he asked her to sing another song of her choice.

After each candidate's performances, the production team wrote down its comments, and Hytner's were in marked contrast to his honeyed words. His standards, I felt, were almost impossibly high, for his notes were devastating: 'Ersatz . . . glamour . . . abominable . . . dreadful . . . not as bad as the pianist . . . ' The habit was catching and I found myself writing of one candidate: 'North Korean prison guard look.' Hytner's comments may have been tough, but they were never gratuitous. 'Batters the song into submission,' he wrote of one, and, 'Savoy Grill voice, but funky interesting face.'

After a batch of auditions, the team, like American football players at the start of a game, huddled together and whispered to each other. At the end of the day, very few of those auditioned found favour in their eyes. 'Too American' or 'brassy voice' were the frequent complaints. Some of the singers were ravishingly beautiful, including an exceedingly young former boat person whom I would have hired on the spot, even if she had not been able to sing a note, but her voice, apparently, 'lacked range'. Mackintosh had one standard, ultimate putdown: 'boring', but he also stepped in to defend a candidate the others dismissed. 'You don't seem to realise how many people there are in this show,' he kept saying. 'Where are they going to come from? I want her on the list.'

The New York casting session, that week in November 1988, was disappointing. And though, in Los Angeles, a few more names were added, there was still no remotely possible *Miss Saigon* among them. The number of candidates was in marked contrast to that at the *Les Misérables* casting session, some years earlier in the same Los Angeles church hall. Then hundreds of performers had taken the place by siege, some of them sleeping in their cars to make sure of an audition the following day.

Hawaii was full of honeymooning Japanese, and the casting team took an instant dislike to the place. Auditioning here was in the American Repertory Theatre, where a well-meaning staffer, clearly unfamiliar with the name of the *Les Misérables* composer, asked Schönberg, in a friendly but somewhat patronising way: 'So your name's Claude-Michel? What should I call you?' Schönberg looked at him with Gallic loathing. 'Just call me maestro,' he replied.

Three people caused Hytner and the production team to put their heads together and whisper excitedly. Janet Stice, part-American, part-Filipino, was learning Japanese, but was determined to pursue a stage career. The auditioning schedule was put aside as Hytner made her sing a second song – 'Think of Me', from *Phantom of the Opera*, with Mackintosh muttering: 'I like her better than some I've seen on stage.' Then Schönberg coached her through the words and music of one of the *Miss Saigon* numbers, alone, while the rest of us waited outside. She learnt the song in twenty minutes, and sang it with considerable emotion. This time, when Hytner said *very good indeed*, he clearly meant it. 'Exciting,' Vincent Liff whispered. The team went into a prolonged huddle. Could this be Kim? Apparently not.

The same routine occurred with Melanie, a part-Japanese University of Hawaii graduate who was teaching dance at a private school. But the real discovery was Chloe Stewart, leggy, adorable, part-Irish, part-Chinese and part-Korean, who sang 'I Don't Know How To Love Him' from *Jesus Christ Superstar*, and bowled everyone over. 'How old are you?' Hytner asked. She was fifteen. After taking her through a *Miss Saigon* number, Schönberg kissed her on the forehead, for the first time the charming, seductive Frenchman. But Mackintosh shook his head. 'We're very impressed,' he said. 'But she's far too young. Equity would never allow it.'

On to Manila, the title role still unfilled. From the start of the trip, Schönberg had predicted that here was where we would find the leading performers. The Philippines, he pointed out, had unique musical traditions. Half the jazz orchestras of Asia were staffed by Filipinos. Singing was in their blood.

He was right. On the first day of casting in Manila, two

candidates dazzled the production team: Lea Salonga and Monique Wilson. After their initial auditions, we all knew the major hurdle had been overcome. Here were not one, but two, potential Miss Saigons. Both were stars in their own right. Lea Salonga, seventeen, a first year student, had started singing in concerts at the age of nine and had extensive film and TV credits. From the very first note of the song she had chosen to sing, Eponine's 'On My Own' from *Les Misérables*, the entire team knew that here was someone special. With George Benson's 'Greatest Love Of All' she confirmed both the range and outstanding quality of her voice.

Lea Salonga

Her close friend, Monique Wilson, eighteen, was also a student, majoring in theatre arts at the University of Manila, but she too was a seasoned performer, with impressive theatrical and singing credits, from *La Cage aux Folles* to *Les Liaisons Dangereuses*. Like other Filipino members later chosen, she was a product of the remarkably professional Philippines Repertory Company, Manila's leading theatre with a record that many European or American theatrical 'ensembles' might envy.

The second day of auditions was disappointing, probably because the production team's sights were now set so high. At the end of the day, we waited for cars to take us to the residence of the American Ambassador, Nick Platt, for a party. Due to Manila's perpetual traffic, the cars were over forty minutes late, and as they arrived, I noticed, out of the corner of my eye, a good-looking girl in stretch pants rushing out of a taxi and into the Philippines Cultural Centre, where auditioning had been taking place. The room where we had been auditioning was now closed. We found a key, but no pianist. 'My name's Jenine Desiderio, and I'm going to sing "MacArthur Park",' she said. Her voice was unforgettable. Then and there, Schönberg decided to take her through the routine of Gigi's song:

> They are not nice,
> they're mostly boys.
> They swear like men,
> they screw like boys.
> I know there's nothing in
> their hearts
> but every time I take one
> in my arms, it starts.

By the time she had finished, the production team knew they not only had two potential Miss Saigons, but also two potential Gigis (Jenine Desiderio later understudied the title role in London with huge success, Isay Alvarez playing Gigi).

The call-backs began on the third day, and once again, the

professionalism of Lea Salonga, Monica Wilson and Jenine Desiderio startled everyone. Monica Wilson's rendering of 'I Swear I'd Give My Life for You', using a cloth bundle in place of a child, had the roomful of people watching close to tears. Her poise was as remarkable off-stage as on. She had seen every Broadway show of note. 'And where did you stay in New York?' Mackintosh asked her. 'In David Merrick's house,' she replied. He was, she explained airily, a family friend.

Lea Salonga demonstrated an ability to learn a song in minutes, sing it flawlessly and hold the stage. Her mother, Feliciana Salonga, accompanied her everywhere, and Mackintosh worried about this. 'Stage mothers frighten me.'

Because of the unexpected wealth of talent, departure was delayed for a day while more *Miss Saigon* numbers were rehearsed. Another promising singer, Tina Agoncello, also made a distinct impression on the final day.

Monique Wilson

Back in London, the mood was now one of elation, and very soon Simon Bowman (Chris), Claire Moore (Ellen), and Peter Polycarpou (John), emerged as obvious front-runners. All had prior Mackintosh connections, Polycarpou and Bowman in *Les Misérables*, Claire Moore in the lead role in *Phantom*. Keith Burns had the looks, build and voice for Thuy, the man Kim was destined to marry, and he, again, had a Mackintosh connection in 'Les Mis'. There remained one major role to fill, that of the Engineer, and here too there was a link with the past, though it was an unfulfilled and largely unknown one.

Jonathan Pryce is a major film actor (*The Ploughman's Lunch, 1984*) who achieved instant fame in his first major London West End theatre part in Trevor Griffiths's *Comedians*. What few outsiders know is that he almost played the lead in *Phantom of the Opera*, for he is also a trained singer. Only conflicting film roles prevented him from auditioning for the part. Hytner, in a casting conference, said of the Engineer: 'It's someone like Jonathan Pryce we need. If only he could sing.' 'He does,' said Boublil, who had seen him in a recent London production of *Uncle Vanya*. For his audition, Pryce sang the 'Willkommen' song from *Cabaret* with such brio that all those present at the London Palladium, where casting sessions were being held, burst into loud, prolonged applause. Pryce, a leading stage and screen star, was the only 'name' in the show, and the announcement that he would be performing in *Miss Saigon* was noted in most of Britain's papers, and in some of them on the front page. In fact his singing role had begun as far back as 1971 as the narrator in the *Caucasian Chalk Circle* but this was to be his first major singing role in London's West End.

Boublil, Schönberg and Mackintosh returned to Manila in early 1989 to seek out eight more people to fill the male roles. By this time they too were front-page news in the Manila newspapers. There was pandemonium at the Cultural Centre, besieged by hundreds of people. 'It was straight out of "Chorus Line",' says Miguel Alvarez, who had been told about the quest for Miss Saigon by friends. He lived in Tacloban City, and almost missed the plane, which was overbooked. 'I was fifteenth on the waiting list but when I explained why I was going to Manila someone gave me their seat.'

'It *was* "Chorus Line" all over again,' Boublil recalls. 'There were scenes of near hysteria when we announced who was to come back for re-auditioning on the final day. Then Cameron had to do the cruellest thing in his life. He said: "I'm going to call certain names. I want to say we are going to call the names of those we unfortunately cannot keep. I also want to say everyone has been wonderful or you wouldn't be here on the last day." He started calling the names and the incredible thing was that the people who were *not* being kept were embracing those who were staying, there was no bitterness, no envy, nothing but joy for the chosen eight. We had expected to remain closeted with those we had selected to discuss their parts and the arrangements for the next few weeks, but as soon as their names were known, there was an uproar, we were swamped by crowds waiting outside. Whole families burst into the audition room. There were tears, huggings, everyone was shouting and crying, those who were not coming seemed as happy as those who *had* been chosen. There was no way we could make ourselves heard. We were all very close to tears that day. I kept saying: we have a plane to catch, and work to do, but it was all to no avail.'

Before they left Manila, those selected staged a farewell concert. Called simply '*The Filipinos of* Miss Saigon', it was televised and attended by a capacity audience that included President Cory Aquino herself. The future cast presented cabaret, songs from Gershwin to Sondheim, with a leavening of numbers from *Les Misérables* and a few from the forthcoming *Miss Saigon* production. They were a remarkably representative cross-section of Filipino society, from the very poor to the very wealthy. Among them was Victor 'Cocoy' Laurel, himself a veteran performer from the Philippines Repertory Theatre and the son of Vice-President Laurel, and Miguel Alvarez, who hadn't actually seen the ad 'because we are too poor to buy newspapers'. There were also some local star performers like Junix Inocian and Bobby Martino who had a considerable following in the Philippines. (Eight months after *Miss Saigon*'s London opening, Jenine Desiderio was understudying Kim and Junix Inocian the Engineer, to considerable acclaim.) There was one unforeseen defection: a few weeks before the Filipino contingent was due to leave for London, Tina Agoncello, a highly talented singer, attended a retreat organised by a fundamentalist 'born-again' Christian sect, became an instant convert, and dropped out: her group refused to allow her to come to London.

Tam – there are always at least three children playing the part in rotation

13 The American Dream

'Vietnam', says Richard Maltby, 'was the dark mirror image of the American Dream. We went over to sell our American values and ended up with every horrible corruption of them imaginable – beginning with the English language: "winning their hearts and minds" meant napalming the village. We tried to put our values to work and, when they didn't work, we forced them on them at all costs whether anybody wanted them or not.' The all-American homespun philosophy which rings so surely through *South Pacific* would have no place in *Miss Saigon*: like Ensign Nellie Forbush, the zonked-out Marines of the Saigon bars and brothels might well be 'high as a flag on the Fourth of July', but for entirely different reasons. Meanwhile, all around, weird distortions of the American way are reflected back at them – in the Engineer's garish suit, in the bar-girls' vision of New York, even in Kim's hopes of a better life for her young son. The Statue of Liberty exercises an extraordinarily powerful pull on many of these people, even if it is a siren song for the pathetically deluded.

The American Dream was obviously going to figure in the show in some form, and, while working out his libretto, Alain Boublil found himself collecting stray magazine and newspaper cuttings which mentioned the phrase, including Michael Dukakis's acceptance of the Presidential nomination at the 1988 Democratic party convention:

> 'My fellow Americans, we're going to win this race. We're going to win because we are the party that believes in the American Dream. A dream so powerful that no distance of ground, no expanse of ocean, no barrier of language, no distinction of race or creed or colour can weaken its hold on the human heart. I know, because I'm a product of that dream.'

As Governor Dukakis was to learn a few months later, the dream does not always come true.

From the outset, then, it seemed to demand a song of its own. 'We must have', said Alain Boublil to Claude-Michel Schönberg, 'something like "*Le rêve Américain*"' – and he sang a setting of the phrase not too different from what the composer eventually produced. This was an eerie plaintive ballad, designed to follow 'The Heat Is On In Saigon' in the opening scene of the show. The beauty contest is over, Gigi has been elected 'Miss Saigon', and

148

now a lottery is being held to see which of the Marines who put money on her will win her for the night. The scene freezes, and Gigi steps forward to sing about '*Le rêve Américain*' because it is, according to Boublil, 'what they should be singing about – and, after all, what is the whole show about?'

So far, so good – in Boublil's original French text. But then, when he and Richard Maltby came to adapt the song, the American stubbornly refused to look for an English equivalent, adamant that, while the rest of the lyric should be translated, the title should remain in French.

'I'm still right,' maintained Maltby, when the subject came up six months after the show's opening.

'I hate it,' said Boublil. 'The idea, in a show in English, of someone suddenly saying "*Le rêve Américain*" – like an Edith Piaf line. And Claude-Michel hated it, too.' Maltby attempted to woo Hytner and Mackintosh, who wavered momentarily before siding with Boublil. His point is well taken: it could easily have seemed like one of those World War II movies where the Nazis say '*Dumkopf*' and '*Schweinehund*' and '*Gott und Himmel*' but conveniently speak in English the rest of the time.

Maltby, however, was convinced that despite the war, most Americans had no idea that in Saigon the bar-girls would have had a smattering of French. Boublil agreed. From seeing films like *Full Metal Jacket*, he reckoned they might occasionally lapse into pigeon-French. He thought, though, that that would be conveyed more plausibly by throwaway lines like Gigi's 'We will make magic, *chéri*' or the Engineer's '*Allez, allez, allez!*' That's the way the Engineer would have spoken, spattering his English with odd phrases of French. But to have had an English song with a strange recurring French title would have been too obtrusive.

Unfortunately, Schönberg's tune wouldn't allow for a straight translation of '*Le rêve Américain*'. '"The American Dream" just didn't fit anywhere in that melody,' says Maltby. 'I tried everywhere, because, as I said to Alain, we can't have a show about the American Dream and not *mention* the American Dream.'

Boublil felt the same. At that time, the two lyricists were working in his Paris apartment and, leaving Maltby to wrestle with the tune, Boublil went out in his car to collect something. Driving past the Porte d'Auteuil Métro, he found himself humming another melody, a big high-kicking Act Two showtune then called '*Je vends tout ce qui s'achete*'. Suddenly, from out of nowhere, Boublil went: '*Da*-da-da-*da*-da-da-*da*, The American Dream!' He went home and told Maltby, 'You know something? It *does* fit somewhere.' So, instead of throwing it away early in Act One, 'The American Dream' became the title of an insinuating Act Two razzle-dazzler, as the Engineer contemplates the impending arrival

of his long-awaited US visa and prepares to kiss off the sex palaces
of Bangkok:

> What's that I smell in the air?
> The American Dream . . .
> Sweet as a suite in Bel-Air,
> The American Dream . . .
> On stage each night: Fred Astaire,
> The American Dream . . .

Thus, a minor detail – the fact that the prosody of '*Le rêve
Américain*' differs from that of 'The American Dream' – caused a
major shift in the score, as the burden of one of the show's principal
themes was moved from the dreamy ballad for which it had been
intended to a completely different style of number. It still, though,
corresponded to Boublil's initial instincts about the drama. 'I'd
always felt,' he says, 'that the Engineer should, in a way, *resolve*
the show, and all the ideas about American materialism.' In retrospect, it would have been throwing away one of your strongest
hands to tackle the subject directly only ten minutes into Act One.

In its finished form, 'The American Dream' is something of a
surprise from the composer of *Les Misérables*. 'It's not my natural
mode of writing,' concedes Schönberg. 'It's a caricature. I wanted
it to sound like the best kind of conventional songs about the
United States. What makes a difference is the orchestration: we
wanted the orchestra to clash, to transform the meaning of the
song completely.' The lyrics have the brash optimistic imagery of
a zillion Broadway anthems:

> Busboys can buy the hotel,
> The American Dream.
> Wall Street is ready to sell
> The American Dream . . .

But the orchestration is supposed to let you know that this whole-
some breeziness is as shabby and sleazy as it could be.

'I had it totally wrong,' says Bill Brohn of his original orchestration. 'At the first workshop, I turned to look at the control
booth and saw Claude-Michel shaking his fists in anger. He's not
one for hiding things, you know. They'd given me plenty of
discussion about the irony in the song, but I'd done it the way I,
as an American, would hear a song about the American Dream.
Instead, it's a European's view of how an Oriental might think
about the American Dream. It was the hardest thing in the whole
show for me. I did another version and missed the mark again.'
'That's a perfectly fine arrangement for a Cy Coleman show,'

Cameron Mackintosh told him, 'but it's not what this moment in this show is. It doesn't have any teeth in it. Go home and listen to Claude-Michel's original tape again.'

Brohn doesn't entirely accept the Cy Coleman label, although he admits he saw it as an uncomplicated hats-and-canes dance number. 'I didn't really get it right until we were in rehearsal,' he says. 'It's an extremely simple melody, but it's a melody that modulates within the course of itself.' In other words, it starts,

> . . . Sweet as a new millionaire,
> The American Dream . . .

then it goes up a semitone:

> Pre-packed ready-to-wear,
> The American Dream . . .

Jonathan Pryce

'Immediately, you're in trouble range-wise,' Brohn explains. 'You can't keep doing that without running into a lot of trouble with voices and instruments, never mind the accompanimental fills between them. But we worked a long time on getting that detuned barrel-house piano sound and those insistent Kurt Weill bass notes, and then intensifying each verse with another overlay of harmonic dissonance. My analogy is with Ravel's "La Valse". Right from the start you know ya got trouble right here in River City, but then the strings come in and you think "Ah, Mantovani, Vienna, gay champagne", and then little by little he turns the thing into a lunatic. I knew that was what we had to try and do with this number, but it's not easy. You run out of ideas, and you run out of instruments. And the problem became even worse when we started staging it, and Bob began finding the spaces for dancing. We had to build the number to what it should be, without ending up like "Busby Berkeley Goes to Hollywood".'

When *Miss Saigon* opened, several first-nighters assumed 'The American Dream' was a deliberate parody of Kander and Ebb, writers of 'New York, New York'. 'But I didn't know them or their work,' says Schönberg. 'Don't forget we only discovered Rodgers and Hammerstein when we opened "Les Mis" in London. I saw the movie of "Sound of Music" when I was a little boy in my little town, but I didn't know it was Rodgers and Hammerstein.' According to Mackintosh, 'He and Alain have learnt a lot since writing the show. But he's still an instinctive composer. He was going for a Kurt Weill or Felliniesque approach to the sort of "New York, New York" songs he's heard on the radio, rather than knowing who wrote "New York, New York" and basing it on that.'

To others at Drury Lane, the relentless vamp and the step-kick in the music evoked 'One Singular Sensation' from *A Chorus Line*, an ironic comparison given that *A Chorus Line*, then in its fifteenth year on Broadway, is Bob Avian's most successful show. For Avian as for Brohn, 'The American Dream' proved a hard nut to crack. He and Hytner knew the number had to be 'bizarre' but other than that they hadn't a clue what to do. 'We get in rehearsal,' says Avian, 'and we start doing what they call a "merry villager" number. You know, you're dealing with people on the street you don't really know, you're trying to give them some identity, but in the end they're still just the chorus singing behind the star. There's no way around it: it was the streets of Bangkok, the same vendors we'd seen in "What A Waste". Nick and I hated it.'

Driving home that night, Avian told Hytner, 'It's in the wrong set. It should be in a crowded bar. Maybe the Engineer's saying goodbye to the night-club.' Hytner slept on that, and said to Avian the following morning, 'You're right. It should be in the bar, but it shouldn't be crowded; it should be late at night and empty.' Avian mulled that over and then took a deep breath: 'Does that mean we can lose the bar and go into his head?' 'Absolutely,' said Hytner. Suddenly, the number was taking off.

Avian took his cue from the lyric references to johns and blondes. The blondes are a glorious apotheosis of the girls the Engineer's been pushing in Saigon and Bangkok: the merchandise is higher quality, but he's still the pimp. As the song started to clarify itself, Avian went back to the title and started to visualise the number in red, white and blue: the Engineer still in his red jacket, the blondes in white, the johns in blue. 'Maybe no one will get it,' he figured, 'but that's what it should be.'

Despite the trappings, though, the Engineer's dreams are as seedy as the reality of his life in Vietnam and Thailand. It's a perversion of the American Dream, made even more lurid by the casting of Jonathan Pryce as the Engineer. At his first stage performance, in a children's competition, Pryce had sung 'My Old Man's A Dustman', but in the years since he had concentrated mainly on non-musical drama. If others were surprised by his singing, Avian was impressed by Pryce's sense of movement. 'He was just what I didn't think he would be. He was very serpentine very fluid. Where I would have gone sharp, he wanted to roll. He loved to turn almost backwards, rather than forwards. So I thought, "Hey, okay. That's taking me somewhere." At first, I'd had an idea for the number where it became *his* dream, and I was going to have a slick guy behind him – a young sharp American version of him. But what would have happened ultimately is that I'd start looking at the younger version as opposed to Jonathan; it would have taken away from him, which I didn't want to do.'

Instead, Avian built the number so that the ensemble acted as a frame for Pryce. 'But he never had to do anything they do, so you'd never know if he was right or wrong. He is a very inventive man anyway, and so he'd change things slightly.'

Some months earlier, talking through the design of the show, John Napier had asked Hytner and Avian, just off the top of his head, if they could use a Cadillac convertible. 'Naaah,' said Avian, and forgot all about it – until he got to the final chorus of 'The American Dream' and discovered he'd exhausted his bag of tricks. That evening, in need of a break, he switched on the TV and was idly flicking across the channels when he came across *thirtysomething*. 'Oh, good, I thought, an American show. I feel like I'm at home. Well, one of the characters gets invited to a party and this big limousine comes to collect her. She steps inside and goes, "Oh, God. The American Dream."'

Rehearsing 'The American Dream'

Instantly, the number fell into place. 'This is what happens,' Avian told Hytner. 'John's Cadillac comes on-stage.' Riding in splendour, in the back seat, is the Engineer's very own 'Miss Chinatown' – dressed as the Statue of Liberty.

As the number builds to its climax, the Engineer starts to writhe deliriously over the hood. 'That was the specific direction I gave him,' laughs Avian. '"Fuck the car."' But, like any other moment of sexual ecstasy, it can't last. The Cadillac and the robotic blondes and johns with their fixed smiles recede into the mists, and the number shrivels away to a solitary dollar bill fluttering to the ground. 'That's just your "ride out". You have to get back to the book, back to reality and out of fantasy.'

It may have been inspired by *thirtysomething*, but, as it turned out, the Engineer's fantasy is not inappropriate to a Bangkok pimp. Long after the number had been completed, Cameron Mackintosh was browsing through a bookshop and came across a volume on Thailand. 'There on the back cover', he said, 'were the King and Queen in exactly the same model of Cadillac. They've had it for fifteen years, they do their royal visits in it. So even that made sense, because they would have been driving around in it and that's where the Engineer could have had the idea.' For Napier and Avian, a moment of serendipity had been retrospectively authenticated.

For reasons other than choreography, 'The American Dream' had proved a difficult time for Avian, and a reminder of at least one seemingly enduring legacy of the Vietnam War: the routine suspicion of American motives, particularly among the young. While working on the number, Nick Hytner had his youthful European and Filipino company improvise what the American

Dream meant to them. 'They're young,' says Avian, 'but it still isn't always nice what they think about America. And, as the only American at those rehearsals, I was sensitive to that. I didn't want to be the ugly American in their eyes, I was trying very hard for everything to be pleasant, but I was getting very upset. I'm first generation, after all. My parents went through the Armenian holocaust, they went through a lot of shit to emigrate to this country, and I'm a result of that. I've achieved success and, as one of the kids said to me, "Well, you are their American Dream." To hear these Europeans' and Filipinos' view of the war was interesting but upsetting. I went there as a performer, big deal, but I had friends who came home with steel plates in their heads. They went through absolute shit and no one even wanted to know what the war was about.'

Bemused by Avian's attitude to the improvisation sessions, Hytner admitted, 'I won't do that in America. I think a younger generation wouldn't find it so much of a problem, but I'm still taken aback by how patriotic Americans are. The show's not anti-American, so much as sceptical about the whole Western success ethos. But it can't afford to get any *more* than sceptical, because after all we're all beneficiaries of it.' Especially, one might add, those members of the company who had made it from first auditions in Manila to the stage of the Theatre Royal: their dreams were perhaps not so very different from Gigi's, Mimi's or Yvette's. From these complex, ambivalent feelings, Hytner, Avian and their cast turned in one of the most memorable numbers of the show – not a contemptuous rejection of 'The American Dream' but a cynical Oriental pimp's own particular angle on it: swirling orchestrations and slithering choreography, as the Engineer exchanges 'Gimme five' palm-slaps with his johns. But the metamorphosis of the song into a seductive parody of Broadway's traditional eleven o'clock showstoppers had still left one problem unresolved: the Act One ballad '*Le rêve Américain*'.

Having transferred 'The American Dream' to the other melody, Boublil and Maltby looked at the lyric as it stood:

> *Le rêve Américain*,
> The dream they leave behind,
> The movie in my mind . . .

'So,' said Maltby, 'you want to call this some stupid title . . . ' – he ran his finger down the lyric – '. . . like "The Movie In My Mind".' 'Exactly,' said Boublil.

Today, Maltby still thinks it's a stupid title which doesn't mean anything. Yet many lyricists would give their eye teeth for it. And, to anybody who doesn't know the story of its tortuous emergence, it's a strong lyric image and absolutely right for the dramatic moment, for the shop-soiled bar-girls and the dreams that linger despite their worldly wisdom:

> The movie in my mind,
> The dream they leave behind,
> A scene I can't erase
> And in a strong GI's embrace
> Flee this life, flee this place.
> The movie plays and plays,
> The screen before me fills.
> He takes me to New York,
> He gives me dollar bills . . .

Despite what Maltby regards as an unsatisfactory compromise, the tune sounds as if it was made for those words. Like most lyricists, he prefers to have the music first, believing that the *right* words for a song are inherent within the melody. 'It's like a Michelangelo statue in the snow,' he says. 'I think the lyric is in the music and you just have to make the effort to dig it out. A lyricist who wrote the lyric first wouldn't think that way.' Maybe not; but a lyricist who wrote the lyric first would at least know that his preferred title – in this case, 'The American Dream' – would fit one of the musical phrases.

Like many happy accidents, though, 'The Movie In My Mind' seems to have a cool logic behind it, connecting the bar-girls and their erstwhile dancing partners, the American servicemen who, back home in the bosom of their families, also have a movie in their minds – as a land they never understood reaches out to haunt them still:

> War isn't over when it ends,
> Some pictures never leave your mind . . .

And sometimes dreams come true, but turn into nightmares somewhere along the way.

14 Rehearsals

The bar-girls in costume

Jenine Desiderio, abroad for the first time in her life, found the London theatre world even more bewildering than London itself. 'There was all this jargon we were completely unfamiliar with,' she recalls. 'People assumed we knew more than we did. The great catchphrase we Filipinos had great fun with was: are you *trained*? The London cast all was. We were not.'

For Hytner, the Asian performers' enthusiasm and excitement were 'the most valuable thing they brought with them, for those with previous experience used it to base their grumbling on.'

Bob Avian, trying to teach the elements of choreography to a cast that included only very few competent dancers, probably had the most difficult time of all. 'In New York this is simply not a problem,' he says. There the world of the American musical theatre is so ultra-competitive that all performers are expected to be able to hold their own in a chorus line. With some exceptions, Avian had to teach basic dance routines. Workouts were held every morning before rehearsals actually began.

Hytner spent the first ten days of rehearsals 'trying to get the company to blend into a whole. We didn't even look at the script or the music for the first two weeks.' Instead, the cast did improvisations, group exercises, separating into groups of four to work on small mini-dramas devised by Hytner. He got them to act out the impressions of Western tourists walking along the seedy Patpong Road area in Bangkok, and then had the same performers go through the same routine, as Asians, aping the Westerners' mannerisms. 'The company wasn't truly blended even by the time previews started,' Hytner recalls. But there was something about the experience and ambition of the Filipinos and their earlier environment that made up for a great deal.

One problem that came to light early on in the rehearsals concerned semi-nudity on stage. It so happened that all the Filipinos in the cast came from staunchly Catholic families. The idea of bumping and grinding away in a sexually seductive way, wearing skimpy bikinis, was something both Mackintosh and Hytner knew they would balk at. 'Here were young people from a chaste and pious Roman Catholic culture coming to late twentieth-century London for the first time where the idea of living through a sensual relationship on stage is no problem,' says Hytner. An innocent conspiracy took place, with the co-operation of all the production team concerned. The costumes for the opening bar scene, and for the Bangkok sequence in the second act, were 'not ready' until the very last minute, just before the dress rehearsal. Even so, 'they came as a real shock to them,' said Hytner, and it took a good deal of eloquence on his part to persuade them to wear them. In the process, he lectured them on the art of the theatre. 'I tried to explain that you don't necessarily have to have three daughters in order to play King Lear.' Suddenly, even the most prudish members of the cast were working out, doing aerobics in their spare time, and even enjoying themselves. 'I suspect', says Hytner, 'that some of the underlying shyness was a lack of confidence in their own bodies.' Once they realised that they looked good, and moved well, their reservations disappeared.

Lea Salonga in the more 'virginal' white shift

One of the key costumes in the show was the result of last-minute improvisation: originally, Lea Salonga, as Kim, was meant to wear a bikini, like the other girls. It did not suit her, and so Andreane Neofitou hastily designed the white shift she wears in the bar scene, which turned out to be a masterly improvement, accentuating her virginal character and singling her out from the other girls in the scene.

One of Hytner's problems, of course, was to give the two Kim players, Monique Wilson and Lea Salonga, an understanding of their roles. 'Lea has no experience of life,' Hytner recalled. 'When rehearsals started she was barely eighteen. She comes from a totally protected environment. It is a fact that she seems incapable of living any emotion without referring it back to her mother.' Stage mothers are a bane for all directors. In the case of Feliciana Salonga, Lea's mother and business manager, Hytner faced a strong-willed, determined person. Though she accepted the rule that only performers were to be allowed inside the theatre, she installed herself in the theatre's bar-coffee shop area and Lea and she would confer whenever the cast would break for rest. 'It took a long time for both Lea and her mother to realise that for the good of Lea's career it had to look as if she was involved in a passionate erotic relationship with a man on the stage,' said Hytner. 'In rehearsals this was a central problem – Lea's unwillingness to allow herself to become a Vietnamese bar-girl intensely involved with a man. I had to get across to Lea – and, perhaps more important, her mother – the notion that whatever Lea did on stage as Kim had nothing to do with what she was really like as a person.'

There were times when Hytner's animated directing had the entire Filipino contingent goggle-eyed. They were flabbergasted, he recalls, when, in frustration and in order to indicate the kind of passion he wanted expressed, he pushed Lea out of the way 'and an astonished Simon Bowman [Chris] found himself rolling around on the bed with me.'

Though the lyrics and music of *Miss Saigon* were almost complete before rehearsals began, work continued on both during the previews and right up to the première. Hytner, who says he's 'never able to look at the text and know exactly what remains to be done' did confer with Boublil and Schönberg on an almost daily basis during the rehearsals.

The 'final' text of *Miss Saigon* used for rehearsals was the eighth draft, but it too became heavily modified during the rehearsal period. On the basis of his practical work as a director, taking the cast through their early paces, Hytner became convinced that the first act was too discursive. Boublil, Maltby and Schönberg agreed with him. 'We've got to simplify this' became a Hytner catchphrase, and minor rewrites of the opening number, 'The Heat Is On In Saigon' were taking place even when the show was in its ninth month, in preparation for its New York opening in April 1991.

David Hersey

The problems with Act Two were not only the Chris–Ellen relationship, but also the timing of the scene where Chris learns that he has fathered Kim's child. Inevitably with such an ambitious show, the views of the production team were not always unanimous: stage designer John Napier, for instance, was not convinced at first of the effectiveness of the filmed back-projection of refugee children during the *bui doi* song, while the rest of the production team, as well as the cast, were bowled over by it. With less than three weeks to go before the first preview, a crisis conference in a private room in the Groucho Club led to Boublil, Maltby and Schönberg rewriting whole scenes and at least two new songs.

A show as complicated to stage as *Miss Saigon* required a vast amount of technical preparation – twelve weeks, in fact. Napier had decided to use a series of 'trucks', which required the stage floor to be completely dug up, and a 'grid' of what looked to a layman like mini-tramlines laid down to enable the various 'trucks' to move in and out of the audience's focus. This in turn required a complicated haulage system of wires powered by hydraulic motors. The helicopter required a chassis, nicknamed 'goalpost' by the production crew. Vertical oriental blinds, all individually controlled, gave the various 'trucks' a required dimension. During the preparations, the whole site was an apparently totally disorganised tangle of wires, cables, pipes and pylons. David Hersey's lighting schedule required the use of not one but three computers.

The immensely influential theatre magazine, *Sightline: The Journal of Theatre Technology and Design*, devoted a special issue to the problems and solutions of staging *Miss Saigon*. As *Sightline* put it, 'John Napier's sets make full use of the huge Drury Lane stage to provide panoramic backgrounds to the principal scenes, many of which are played out downstage on a series of trucks which arrive from upstage on the wings. The main stage area is defined by a U-shaped grid, marked out at floor level by a light curtain. From it hang oriental screens which are raised from time to time to open up the complete stage area. Colour is limited, reserved for a few spectacular moments. Flying brings in black-and-white photographic banners for wartime Saigon, garish lightbox street signs for the brothels of Bangkok. The six pylons which track on and off have many functions, from creating a war-zone landscape to supporting triumphant Vietcong banners; the upstage lift, too, as well as acting as a helicopter launchpad, becomes both US headquarters and an American bedroom.

'The onstage arrival and departure of the helicopter is only part of a flying and trucking sequence which over seven hectic minutes achieves the quality of a black-and-white newsreel film, constantly shifting focus and viewpoints. Twenty seconds after the audience has been gripped by a stage full of actors and scenery in full flight, the area has been cleared to accommodate the "truck" of Kim's room in Bangkok. These sudden contrasts lend the show much power, as do the several moments when Hytner risks cliché to send his principals on the long walk up a bare stage into a romantic fade.' Despite the constant visual excitement and movement of *Miss Saigon* (Boublil noted that Hytner is a director who just won't let his characters become static), Napier insists that 'nothing is there for gratuitous special effects'.

In the case of the Theatre Royal, Drury Lane, the most intractable problem was that of the inclination of the stage to allow the trucks to slide into place. 'You're defying gravity,' says Napier. 'The weight varies according to whether it's going up or down.' Inevitably, the sheer complexity of the staging, and its largely computerised operation (the only device that relied solely on human hands was the joystick-operated helicopter machinery) led to endless breakdowns. 'With people, if you get it wrong, you just start again,' says Hytner. 'A computer will simply bring everything to a halt, and you won't know why.' So frequent were the initial breakdowns that Hytner, in something of a huff, ordered the entire company out of the theatre for a week to allow the technical production team to iron out the many computer problems while they continued to rehearse elsewhere. The computers were necessary because there was so much involved, says Hytner. 'The production manager, Simon Opey, fought a heroic battle, and I'm sorry I lost my cool. It's taught me that I'll use as little high-tech' equipment as possible in any of my future shows.' A serious accident was narrowly avoided at one of the final dress rehearsals when a giant Ho Chi Minh statue kept moving after it should have stopped, almost crushing Shukubi Yo's (one of the bar-girls) foot. She screamed and stagehands rushed onstage, to prevent both a serious injury and the possible destruction of the 'truck' element containing Kim's bedroom shack. Two previews were cancelled while a thorough overhaul took place.

Andreane Neofitou

Costumes and props were the responsibility of Andreane Neofitou and her assistant, Charlotte Bird, and theirs was not an easy task. For *Les Misérables*, Neofitou had gone to the invaluable Victoria & Albert Museum library, which houses nineteenth-century periodicals and etchings of every conceivable type of dress. For *Miss Saigon* they turned to *Paris-Match*, Reuter and BBC photo archives, and the considerable resources of leading costumiers like Berner's, who also maintain their own costume library. There were problems concerning uniforms – not those of the Americans, but those of the Vietcong and the North Vietnamese. A few small liberties were taken with absolute historical accuracy in order to provide a little colour and variety, though Andreane Neofitou insists that the head-dresses worn by some of the Vietnamese are similar to those worn by Cambodian tribesmen fighting with the North Vietnamese. There were problems, too, involving badges of rank and uniform patterns of the post-war Vietnamese army. Neofitou and Bird enlisted the help of the London-based Vietnamese Embassy which in turn recommended that they ask Leon Bartlett, the owner of a travel agency specialising in travel to Vietnam, and his Vietnamese-born wife, Nguyen, for additional assistance. Saigon veterans may remember her: she was receptionist-manageress of the famous wartime New York Bar and Restaurant on Hai Ba Trung, and later managed the Blue Moon bar near the Indian temple just off Tu Do (now renamed Dong Coi) street. Both travel frequently to Vietnam, and they brought back shoes, sandals, pith helmets and even army badges and authentic '33' 'Made in Vietnam' brand beer bottles. Since some of these artefacts were held up in transit through Manila, the cast was performing in costumes that – for the previews – were either incomplete or, later, completely changed.

Neofitou, a perfectionist, was working on costumes right up to the week of dress rehearsals, and a display of what the cast was to wear led to a fairly acrimonious scene only a few days before the first preview performance. Bob Avian insisted the shoes of the cast were all wrong for dancing in and most of the cast complained they were uncomfortable to wear. Hytner and Mackintosh wanted a more natural look, and criticised the costumes for looking too new. 'Thuy's white suit,' says Mackintosh, 'made him look like the captain of "Loveboat".' There were also objections to the tourists' look in the Bangkok scenes. In order to typify them, there were lederhosen for the Germans and seersucker suits for the Americans, and Mackintosh felt this was wrong. He wanted a more 'natural' look, and less clichéd labelling. 'For "Miss

Saigon"'', Mackintosh says, 'everything had to look real: theatricality was out. Some of the original costumes, I felt, looked like a bad tour production of "Kismet".'

The matter was settled within a few days, but not before new sets of shoes had been ordered, the lederhosen discarded and a shopping expedition made to an Oxfam store for second-hand clothing.

For Boublil, Schönberg, Maltby and Bill Brohn, the process of rewriting during rehearsals was an integral part of the rehearsals themselves. 'I have no sense of proprietorial "ego" about my music,' says Schönberg, 'I'm not working for myself, I'm working for the show. If the show is good, I'll be a good composer. If the singer or the staging are not right, I'll be a bad composer – even if the music remains the same. If, during rehearsals, I'm told that something is not working, and I'm convinced the criticism is justified, I'll have no hesitation in making a U-turn. It's the show that counts.'

Because both Boublil and Schönberg welcome a 'hands on' director, they responded favourably to Hytner. 'There was no real Act Two crisis,' says Schönberg. 'What happened was part of the normal rehearsal process. The Bangkok hotel room scene, as it was originally written, was not working. Ellen's song was a disappointment. The problem was inherent in the story, and in the character of Ellen herself. Ironically, this had been Puccini's problem, too, with Kate Pinkerton.'

Claire Moore (Ellen)

Ellen's song went through several stages, the final version substantially altering the thrust of the story, as well as throwing new light on Ellen's feelings and character.

The continuous process of adaptation and invention, even after rehearsals had begun, was a surprise for Bill Brohn. 'There isn't the same collaboration or anything like the questioning and democratic process that I experienced on "Miss Saigon",' he says. 'During rehearsals, for two key numbers, "Bangkok" and "The American Dream", we kept rewriting, right up to and including the previews. By this time we knew the action taking place on the stage, second by second. Some of it was a question of key changes, but for "Bangkok" and "The American Dream" it was more than that: we had to emphasise the change of pace in "Bangkok" coming as it did after several dramatic scenes; for "The American Dream", my original orchestration had been too brassy, too "American".'

For the concluding few bars of the show, Schönberg and Brohn had worked out three orchestration alternatives, which they tried out on three successive preview nights. 'The first sounded like a bull in a china shop,' says Schönberg. 'The second was too complicated.' The third one 'really worked', and was adopted as the definitive ending. Throughout these final rewrites, nine music copyists were working round the clock to provide the orchestra with the amended sheet music.

Nine months before the projected Broadway opening, another rehearsal, of a kind, was taking place. In New York, John Napier started work on a substantially amended set for the Broadway Theatre version. Because of its smaller backstage size, substantial modifications were essential, and both Napier and Hytner, egged on by Mackintosh, took this opportunity to streamline, and to some extent simplify, some of the stage action and scenery changes.

Back in London, for three months before *Miss Saigon* formally opened, double-decker buses had been displaying eight different sets of experimental 'busback posters', while the advertising firm, Dewynters, pondered over their effectiveness. Eventually, shortly before the London première, a definitive choice was made. The final *Miss Saigon* logo, the now famous, impressionistic Chinese brushwork helicopter, designed by Russ Eglin, who has worked with Cameron Mackintosh for over twenty years, soon became so well known to Londoners that it did not require a title.

By opening night, the Theatre Royal, Drury Lane, was fully booked for months ahead. Expectations were high. All those involved in *Miss Saigon* felt they had a hit on their hands.

Outside the Theatre Royal

15 Countdown to Opening Night

A few months before the opening of *Miss Saigon*, Andrew Lloyd Webber opened *Aspects of Love*. 'Did you see that piece in *Variety*?' he said to me, with weary indignation, during previews. '"You can't out-hype Andrew." What do they mean? We haven't advertised anywhere. It's Cameron who's been buying all the bus sides.' In fact, more than a few London Transport Routemasters carried posters for *Aspects*, but that still left plenty over for *Miss Saigon*. Thanks principally to Russ Eglin's logo, by August 1989 the successor to *Les Misérables* was one of the most eagerly awaited events in theatre history. Yet, at the same time, many in the industry took it for granted: no matter how high the box-office advance climbed, there was a sense that for a Cameron Mackintosh musical this was the norm.

'I keep telling people,' sighed Mackintosh, 'that "Miss Saigon" is the first of my shows to open with a really enormous advance, as indeed "Aspects" was for Andrew. These five-million-pound jobs only started with these two. "Phantom" opened with just under a million, "Cats" and "Les Mis" with buttons. But, because "Cats" went to New York, was a big success and became a worldwide hit, and "Les Mis" came out of the woodwork and joined it, and then "Phantom" became a mega-hit, the next two – "Aspects" and "Miss Saigon" – were both looked on to be equal or toppers. But the hype isn't our hype, it's the newspaper hype: it's actually the hype hyping the hype, and that's what all the stories are about.'

That said, Mackintosh has a real showman's flair for, in the slogan of a British insurance company, 'making a drama out of a crisis'. For technical reasons, one of *Miss Saigon*'s preview performances was cancelled – an event which might have prompted a slew of newspaper pieces about whether or not the show was in trouble. (Journalists always pay inordinate attention to cancelled previews, even though it's a time-honoured theatrical convention dating back at least as far as 1879, when the Kiralfy Brothers postponed the first Broadway performance of *Enchantment* because their spectacular scenic effect, the set for the Land of the Ephemerals, had run amok.) Instead, though, the columns were filled with an entirely different story.

In West End houses, although the producer has control of the merchandising – the souvenir brochures, T-shirts, cast albums – the actual programme falls under the control of the theatre owners. Stoll Moss, Mackintosh's landlords at Drury Lane, were charging

£1.20 for *Miss Saigon* programmes, a price the producer considered far too high. As previews of the show got under way, Mackintosh himself turned up on the steps of the Theatre Royal to hand out free cast-lists to members of the audience. Initially taken aback by the extraordinary sight of a theatrical producer picketing his own show, Stoll Moss quickly retaliated by threatening legal action. Mackintosh then announced that he would ban the company from selling T-shirts or any other merchandise in the Drury Lane foyer. Stoll Moss received this news with equanimity: they may lose money, but he would, too, wouldn't he? It was obviously a silly bluff. A few days later, a new shop called Theatre Plus mysteriously appeared just across the street from the Drury Lane lobby, packed to the rafters with *Miss Saigon* goodies. The man behind it, of course, was Cameron Mackintosh.

There are serious issues lurking here. At the time, the chairman-ship of the Australian-owned Stoll Moss had just passed from that old-fashioned showbiz entrepreneur Louis Benjamin into the hands of the company accountant, Roger Filer. As well as Drury Lane, Filer controls the Palladium, Victoria Palace, Her Majesty's and eight other West End houses – a domination of the London theatre not all producers regard as healthy. Few, though, would have the stomach for a protracted fight over such a peripheral issue as the price of the programme, or be happy to chat about it so openly and cheerily as Mackintosh did on Ned Sherrin's *Loose Ends* radio show the weekend before opening. In these grim days of grey 'cheque-book' producers, Mackintosh is, deliberately or other-wise, one of the most quotable men in showbusiness, and his personal intervention in the Stoll Moss dispute ensured that this alleged rip-off, one of many which attend a big musical night out these days, was not blamed on the show.

At the same time, Mackintosh arranged two 'promenade' matinées of *Miss Saigon*, offering the chance to see the hottest show in town at bargain-basement prices. 'Those were two of the best, most exciting performances of the show I've ever seen,' he remembers. 'The people with expense accounts didn't want to queue, they didn't have chauffeurs available on Saturday afternoon, and so the real public went in at a price they could afford. Don't forget that the reason "Aspects" and "Miss Saigon" got such vast amounts of money up front is that the British public had been badly stung by the touts. Not only were they having to pay above the odds to see "Cats" and "Les Mis", but, for the first two years of the run, the touts were selling those high-price tickets to the high rollers, the sort of people who fill Glyndebourne, the execu-tive trips from Japan and all over the world, what I call the new *non*-audience. Not the real theatre-lovers.'

For whatever reasons, the combination of theatre-lovers, touts and 'the new non-audience' had helped stack up a £5 million advance for *Miss Saigon* – and it was from this position of strength that he was able to embark on his feud with Stoll Moss. Show *business* is notorious for its shoddy, short-sighted compromises, but Mackintosh is not, temperamentally, the sort of man to fall grudgingly into line – as the New York theatre community was soon to discover.

But, if a huge advance is good for the biz, where does it leave the show? Addressing his cast before the opening performance on 20 September, Nick Hytner assured them that 'the only people who aren't our friends have already written their reviews – and, even if they haven't, it doesn't matter what they say anyway because this show's sold out.' Hytner may be right in the unimportance of the critics on a show like *Miss Saigon*, but his words on the impregnability of a big advance need to be taken with a pinch of salt. In recent seasons, the huge advances for *Ziegfeld* (in the West End) and *Legs Diamond* (on Broadway) evaporated within weeks, as audiences discovered the shows weren't all they were hyped up to be. Andrew Lloyd Webber likes to point out that, in real terms, the largest advance ever was for Irving Berlin's *Mr President*, which, after all the ballyhoo, spluttered and died after only a few months. 'Hype will only go so far,' says Mackintosh. 'What makes a show a success is the word of mouth.' You could forgive a producer who's taken £5 million up front a degree of complacency, but Mackintosh and his creative team were beavering away until the very last moment.

A week before the opening, I went to Drury Lane to meet Richard Maltby. The would-be theatre-goers, spending their lunch hours waiting patiently in line just in case there were a couple of upper circle restricted view seats available before 1992, paid no attention to the amiable American strolling through the lobby. He looked like one of those tourists who clog up the Tube and stand on the wrong side of the escalator. Little did they know that burning a hole in his rucksack were the latest rewrites on the hottest lyrics in town. And, even if they had known, they'd probably have been surprised to find anybody still fussing over what was already a guaranteed hit.

'I wanted to be a set-designer, not a lyric-writer,' Maltby told me that day. 'But no one at school was interested in musicals, so in order to have everyone see my scenery I had to write the show. On "Miss Saigon" we decided last week that one scene was too long. The music cuts took ten minutes, but it took Alain and me an entire weekend to end up with a scene which says exactly what we said before but in half as many lines, none of which have the same beats as the lines in which the thoughts were originally expressed. You kill yourself and everyone says, "That's easy. You just made a few cuts." That's why I hate lyric-writing.'

Besides, no matter how good the words are, they can still get lost – often because of the problems accruing from sound amplification. 'When you get into the theatre', says Bill Brohn, 'the lighter and the stager become much more important in focusing on *who* is singing. But, more often than not, the reason lyrics don't get heard is because of the tendency in young performers to rely on the microphone to clarify bad diction. The microphone does not improve diction, it only amplifies the mush that's put into it – or, in the case of Jonathan Pryce, the wonderful articulation that's put into it. There is the lesson if these young people would just listen to it.'

In the main, these are technical problems – a question of working a particular performer a bit more, or balancing the sound differently. But it's also at this fairly late stage, when the performers are heard with the orchestra for the first time, that more complex problems are revealed: what if the actor's and the orchestrator's interpretation don't match? 'Claude-Michel and I did a lot of work on the Engineer's numbers,' Brohn says, 'but then, when Jonathan took the role and began building it with Nick, some of our choices proved to be wrong.' Brohn cites the scene in Act One when the Engineer tries to force a visa out of Chris:

> We had a deal for Kim
> But that's on ice . . .
> I'm sorry, Sergeant,
> But I've changed the price . . .

The Engineer, Schönberg said, 'must be like a sneaky little Oriental mouse at this point.' Brohn went to work and produced 'what I thought was one of my better passages: I had two piccolos going together and a couple of other interjections like that. But, as Jonathan shaped the scene in rehearsal, I felt more and more uneasy about what I'd done. It's too parody Oriental. When you look at Jonathan, you'd never think of a mouse. So it was wrong for him, and it's still in there.' The offending sequence passes in a few seconds; it would have been expensive to change that late in the day; but to a perfectionist like Brohn it was still an irritant.

None the less, these are minor nip-and-tuck jobs compared to the wholesale surgery being performed on most shows at this stage. Oscar Levant once defined the musical as 'a series of catastrophes ending in a floorshow', a summation which seems at its most pertinent in the run-up to opening night. In America, this perilous period has accumulated its own vocabulary, a dictionary of permanent crisis management: a musical 'in trouble' calls in a 'doctor' to 'fix' the show. Too often, as general panic sets in,

166

whatever the original impulse for doing the show was gets obliterated. During rewrites, James Goldman, author of *Follies*, always pins a large note on his bathroom mirror: 'What is this play about?' It's a reminder, as the pressure hots up, not to lose his grip.

By these standards, the previews of Mackintosh's musicals are remarkably free of headless chickens – especially considering the shorter run-in period. 'We did not have the advantage of going out of town,' he says noting that every Broadway smash of the last forty years – *My Fair Lady, Hello, Dolly!, Fiddler On The Roof* – underwent substantial changes on the road. 'I consider that we're remarkably blessed that a gigantic piece of very difficult material cohered as much as it did in what was only an eight week rehearsal period and two weeks of previews.'

'We're not here to enjoy it,' Schönberg likes to say. 'We're here to suffer it. It's a foolish dream to imagine that writing a musical is going to be easy.' Four years earlier, when he and Boublil had begun laying out the book of the show, they had seen *Miss Saigon* as a small, intimate love story. 'Then one day we wanted to describe why Chris left Kim in Saigon – not because he was a bastard, but because he *couldn't* take her with him. And we decided we had to see the fall of the city, with the Americans flying their helicopters and the people on the pavement in front of the Embassy – like that famous photo. The subject is always stronger than you are.'

Evacuation of the US Embassy on stage at the Theatre Royal, and in Saigon, 1975

As John Napier manoeuvred his white Cadillac and helicopter into place and Bob Avian marshalled his corps of marching Vietcong, that intimate little love story could easily have been buried. 'When we were in the room writing,' says Maltby, 'Alain and I realised that virtually every scene was a two- or three-scene: never more than two or three characters. What you see on the stage is this great canvas, which Nick uses brilliantly to support what's still a very intimate love story.' You could, possibly, do *Miss Saigon* with a cast of six, but there's no doubt that the drama is all the more intense for being in constant danger of being swept up by the great human tide around it. Even in their most private moments, these characters, you feel, are never really alone: in Ho Chi Minh City, there are always eyes peering out of the darkness round every corner, behind every hovel. It's an inspired use of the chorus the writers could never have foreseen.

Yet, in a sense, it was all there on the original tape. 'Working with the *right* people doesn't always mean working with the most celebrated people,' says Schönberg. 'It means working with people who belong to your show. Nick and Cameron and the rest may surprise us, but they are still people for whom the same words mean the same thing.' Most of the epic elements, including the helicopter, were there in the script, because 'it's always better to show something than to tell it,' but there were a few adjustments. Boublil and Schönberg had seen the Vietcong victory celebrations in Ho Chi Minh City culminating in a fireworks display. Because of safety regulations, that proved impossible, so instead the giant statue of Uncle Ho was substituted.

Looking back over the long gestation period, Schönberg says, 'At the beginning, my job is very difficult, because I'm writing an abstraction: I am finding a *sound* for a story. But, when we go into rehearsal, the music is about eighty per cent there. With the lyrics, only about forty per cent is fixed – because, when you run into a problem, everybody uses words to talk with, so it seems easier to complain about the words, to say, "These lyrics aren't right," rather than, "This is the wrong melody."' It's an assessment, Boublil and Maltby would heartily endorse. For all that, though, the twenty per cent of the music which wasn't fixed caused the composer a few wobbles. After what he calls 'a crisis meeting', twenty minutes of Act Two were slung out, including a song for Chris's wife Ellen:

> What if he doesn't come back home tonight?
> She is so beautiful, a man just might . . .
> But I know him,
> That love for her
> Was long ago . . .
> But if he doesn't come back home tonight . . .
> What if he doesn't come back home tonight?

For what it's worth, I'm rather partial to the ballad, but I have to admit that my opinion's not widely shared. Bob Avian took to referring to it as 'Ellen's country-and-western number', and singing the lyric in a Tammy Wynette accent. 'Cameron,' he'd begin, 'when Ellen does that song, "What if he doesn't come back to *the hotel room* tonight . . . ?"' – pointing out an awkward blemish in the title: it's hard to imagine anywhere less homely than the bland international hotel suite in Bangkok in which she had to deliver the number. 'Nobody ever liked it,' says Hytner. 'It was the wrong number, it doesn't ring true. It's "Would you now kindly shed a tear for this poor woman?", not "What does this woman really feel like?"'

'I was very scared,' Schönberg remembers. 'I faced the wall and said, "Now I have to write a new song." I'm not very comfortable in that position. I never know if it's going to come or not.' Luckily, it came – in a ballad of controlled self-knowing defiance:

> In her eyes, in her voice,
> In the heat that filled the air

Part of him still lingers there.
I know what pain her life today must be
But if it all comes down to her or me
I won't wait, I swear
I'll fight . . .

'What excites me,' said Maltby, as the previews proceeded, 'is
that we can bring a helicopter on the stage and show the fall of the
city, but it's topped by an emotional moment – which is actually
a triple emotional moment: the girl sees the wife, the wife says
"Oh, my God. Okay. Who do you love?" and he opens up for
the first time, and what he says is just devastating.' Unlike so
many other mega-musicals – those ponderous gargantuans which
prompt the familiar quip from cynics that they came out whistling
the set – *Miss Saigon* looked as if it was going to deliver an
emotional charge to match anything the set-builders could come
up with.

In the run-up to opening, however, a few lines strayed into the
show from pens other than Boublil's and Maltby's. As Jonathan
Pryce got the measure of his role as the Engineer, he took to
rearranging some of the lines, including:

Claire Moore in rehearsal

> That bridal gown gives you some class.
> Lower your eyelids as you pass.

And then adding one of his own:

> Men pay a lot for virgin ass.

As Pryce later told me with mischievous pleasure, not only were
his lines striking enough to be quoted in one of the reviews but
the critic in question presented them as evidence of 'the dismal
predictability of Alain Boublil and Richard Maltby Jnr's lyrics'.
Doubtless, the authors were relieved they hadn't accepted any
other libretto contributions from him.

Steering a musical through to its first night can take its toll, but,
on this occasion, according to Bob Avian, 'Cameron, Nick and I
were always laughing. We wound up having such a great time
on this show, we were like the Three Stooges.' This agreeable
atmosphere was due to Mackintosh's painstaking preparation, but
it was also proof of his uncanny instincts as a matchmaker: all his
unlikely 'marriages' – Hytner and Avian, Boublil and Maltby –
seemed to be working out. When I asked him once why he put
together such strange bedfellows, he would only say, 'You can't
have the same people doing the same show in a different guise all
the time. You'll get found out.' On 20 September, at least part of
the excitement stemmed from the sheer novelty: Jonathan Pryce's

169

first musical, Nicholas Hytner's first musical, Lea Salonga's West End début, and so on.

On the opening night, Hytner, a lone lounge suit in a sea of black ties, announced to enquiring pressmen that he would not actually be seeing the performance. Instead, he passed the evening peering pensively from the top of the Theatre Royal's extravagant central stairwell. 'I never watch opening nights,' said Avian. 'I'm always in some bar around the block. But this time I couldn't leave the theatre. I didn't have a seat, I was standing at the back and I was crying more than anybody.' This was quite a claim. From where I sat in the stalls, most of the second act was continually underscored by muffled sobs. As Lea Salonga took her bows and the cheers threatened to blow the roof off, it was almost as if the applause was a necessary catharsis – a way for the audience to release the great flood of emotion which had welled up during the drama's final tragic moments.

'Although I suspect standing ovations because they are usually stage-managed by enthusiastic backers,' wrote Milton Shulman in the following day's *Evening Standard*, 'the roar of approval at Drury Lane last night was the most spontaneous acclaim I have heard at a first night since the opening of *My Fair Lady*.' For Mackintosh, no comparison could have been more flattering: he regards Lerner and Loewe's adaptation of *Pygmalion* as the perfect musical. For Avian, too, the harrowing final scene was part of a distinguished tradition: 'Death seems to work in musicals. You'd think it was the last thing you'd want to do, but look at "West Side Story", "The King and I" and now "Miss Saigon". They all end tragically in death – and they all work just great!'

When the cheers finally died away and the house emptied, a thousand guests were ferried by river boats to a lavish celebration (Vietnamese cuisine, naturally) in the shadow of Tower Hill – a procession as bizarre as anything seen on stage, of creators and cast, friends and celebrities, and gossip columnists and photographers, whose newspapers nowadays devote as many column inches to coverage of the first-night party as they do to an analysis of the show itself. On Broadway, the critics attend previews rather than the official opening night, write their reviews in advance and have them ready for the first editions – which usually means the notices arrive when the party's in full swing and, if they're unfavourable, clear the room quicker than a nuclear warning, as the glitterati head for the hills, leaving only a trail of trampled crudités behind them. In London, happily, first night reviews are still reviews of the first night, and, as a result, are still being barked down the phone to copy-takers as the revellers assemble: there are no brutal critical dissections to cast a pall over the carousing. The critics, like the hangovers, belong to the morning after.

The first to arrive reflected the eccentric preoccupations of their own newspapers. 'Fergie will absolutely love this expensive new musical because the biggest star of the show is a helicopter,' chirruped Maureen Paton in the opening sentence of her *Daily Express* notice. This was a reference to a children's book by the Duchess of York, a children's book about a cheeky chopper called Budgie. When she eventually turned her attention to the musical itself, Miss Paton confidently declared that 'no real tunes emerge despite the snatches of melody in the rock ballads'. Another tabloid, *Today*, was equally certain: 'A disappointing follow-up to the spectacular *Les Misérables*.' In the *Daily Telegraph*, Charles Osborne thought the show a cynically concocted 'product', and adopted a cod Chevalier accent as he speculated on the authors' plotting: 'We must 'ave a big show-stoppair 'ere, while ze girl ees waiting to keel 'erself. *N'est ce pas?*'

After that, everything came up roses. According to Michael Coveney in the *Financial Times*, 'The music has a wonderful ungoverned romantic spirit – you never know how any number is going to end – backed up by Oriental string arrangements and brassy walls of flat-out orchestration . . . Bob Avian's musical staging comes into its own with goose-stepping Chinese military, or Vietnamese street girls . . . Throughout the evening, Lea Salonga as Kim sings her socks off, and the dedication to her son is one of the most moving things I have ever seen on the London stage. She is an amazing talent.'

Miss Saigon, wrote the *Daily Mail*'s Jack Tinker, 'has both the courage and the compassion to confront the brutal facts of its situation with a commendably small attempt to decorate the tale with the trappings with which musicals usually sugar unpleasant pills.' This theme – the pleasant discovery of worthwhile drama in a form which invariably trivialises its subjects – was also taken up by Michael Billington in the *Guardian*: 'A musical about Vietnam? I confess I approached *Miss Saigon* at Drury Lane with trepidation reinforced by a correspondent who complained of racial and sexual stereotypes. What I found was an unusually intelligent and impassioned piece of popular theatre: revamped Puccini with a sharp political edge . . . You obviously do not go to a musical for detailed political analysis; and when Kim sang: "Do you want to hear how my village was burned?" I was tempted to answer: yes. But both Schönberg (who has written a powerful score full of deliberate Puccini echoes) and Boublil have produced a musical that addresses a modern tragedy with seriousness and integrity. It is rare and refreshing to find popular theatre that relates the personal to the political.'

With few exceptions, the Sundays continued the bouquets, with even an unimpressed Michael Ratcliffe in the *Observer* relishing the players' efforts: 'Pryce gives a gorgeous performance, with the slightly parodic pleasure of the classical actor who always wanted to sing and dance.' *Miss Saigon*, said John Gross in the *Sunday Telegraph*, 'is an undoubted triumph of its genre – a much better musical, in my opinion, than *Les Misérables* . . . If a single prize were to be awarded, however, it would have to go to the director, Nicholas Hytner – and his designer, John Napier, would have a good claim to be runner-up. Between them, they have devised a stunning series of theatrical effects which are more than just theatrical in the narrow sense. Their *tour de force* is a recreation of the pull-out from Saigon, complete with a descending and departing helicopter. You admire their virtuosity, but not so much that you don't also register something of the panic and misery of the Vietnamese who have been left behind, held back by the wire-mesh gates.'

For most of these critics, *Miss Saigon* was an agreeable surprise: at last, all the paraphernalia of the modern high-tech mega-musical were being deployed in the service of drama. Remove the snobbery in some of these heavyweight reviews, and they're a resounding vindication of the creative team's ambitions. 'A musical', said Richard Maltby, 'is always sailing between Scylla and Charybdis. It's a popular entertainment for an audience, which it must always be, but it can also involve thought-provoking elements and in some cases the highest issues of playwriting. Sometimes you veer too closely to one side or the other, and then you have to try and get back on course. How you do that is the art.'

A few years ago, Alan Jay Lerner wrote, 'The Theatre Royal, Drury Lane, the best and most popular musical theatre extant, is nevertheless not the setting for experimental theatre.' Yet, looked at from a variety of different angles, *Miss Saigon* was an experiment. Most musicals are set either in the rosy-hued cloisters of nostalgic memory or in a past sufficiently remote not to distress us. 'Nick and I were talking about it the other day,' said Cameron Mackintosh after the opening. 'We've pulled off something very few people have pulled off: a huge *contemporary* smash-hit musical, which does affect audiences and does entertain at the same time.' For some of his team, the uniqueness of the show was more personal. Musing on the massive advance, Richard Maltby realised, 'I've never had an opening night where, the next morning, I didn't get up and hope someone would be in the theatre that evening.' He smiled. 'I guess this way's not so bad, though.'

16 Back to Work

'I did a lot of research,' said Jonathan Pryce in the *Independent* a week before opening, 'and I found that people in Saigon at that time did, in fact, sing everything.' There is more to this joke than meets Pryce's heavy-lidded Oriental eye-piece (the ones which were soon to prove so controversial). For at least a few of us, the most interesting question in musical theatre at that time was whether 'singing everything' meant automatically abandoning reality. The through-composed musical gets by on subjects like *Phantom of the Opera* because we're prepared to accept lush declarative tunes, flowery lyrics and general swanning about from larger-than-life figures entirely removed from our own lives – the sort of shows, to quote Broadway producer Lee Shubert's brute dismissal of costume drama, where people write letters with feathers. But are we doomed to a diet of *Phantoms*, or can the form grapple with contemporary characters who speak normally and wear modern dress? 'That was the gamble,' says Mackintosh. 'I knew every bit of it had to be *real*.'

'Call him Chris, he'll like that'

For me at least, this was *Miss Saigon*'s most impressive achievement. Worn down by the simple-minded pop pageantry of British musicals, I doubted whether the form could embrace such a grim, naturalistic environment. But Boublil and Schönberg seized the bones of the Puccini plot and gave them a modern dress which fitted effortlessly: the grand passions of opera set to the less florid idioms of the everyday world, the sweep of Puccini fused with the naturalism of the American musical play. If only because of this coalescence of two traditions, *Miss Saigon* is one of the most hopeful and significant developments in the new school of musical theatre – although I have to confess, whenever I've burbled on in similar vein to the writers concerned, they've studiously avoided rising to the bait. 'I cannot answer that,' Alain Boublil said. 'When you're writing a show,' added Richard Maltby, 'you don't sit down and write a breakthrough. You write what you think is best for the show. I never had the slightest doubt that "Miss Saigon" could be as tough as it wanted – so long as you don't assume that just because it's dark and important the audience'll be interested. They're not, you're not, I'm not. Obviously there has to be more to it than that. But, from my experience of musicals, "Miss Saigon" is set in the middle of the main road.'

That's a judgment shared by *Miss Saigon*'s detractors, to whom the musical was just another exercise in slick showbiz manipulation. 'The theatre is *about* manipulation,' responded Mackintosh.

173

'I just believe you should do it with as much integrity as possible.' Certainly, all *successful* musicals are about manipulation and all the great showmen – George Abbott, Jerome Robbins, Bob Fosse, Michael Bennett – are master manipulators, harnessing the music, text, choreography and other disparate elements to the emotional bond between the audience and the show, a bond far stronger than in most straight plays. If it wasn't manipulative, it would be incoherent, or, as they say on Broadway, it wouldn't *work*. 'It's very manipulative when King Lear comes on with his dead daughter in his arms,' maintains Nick Hytner. 'Incredibly manipulative. If people seriously imagine that Shakespeare didn't know that would make the audience cry, they're mad. But he also felt profoundly involved in that moment. He felt it was *true*. Well, I think Alain and Claude-Michel feel that what they're doing is true. All people mean when they say something is manipulative is that they weren't convinced of its truth.'

In fact, when you pressed these critics further, it usually transpired that what they really meant was that *Miss Saigon* wasn't manipulative enough – at least in the political sense. In the early weeks of the London run, some visitors from the US found it too hard on the Americans, others felt that it let them off the hook too easily. To a British audience, Vietnam had few personal resonances – and, even if you were to find a comparable overseas débâcle, the opportunity to wallow in imperial guilt has been a staple attraction of the English theatre for thirty years. The New York audience, though, has never exhibited a similar taste for self-flagellation. Could it be that *Miss Saigon* was too controversial to be a hit on Broadway? Over dinner, I asked Bob Avian if he wasn't worried. 'Controversy is like fatness: it happens,' he said laconically, using an analogy I didn't fully understand – particularly as he'd just declined dessert, while I was stuffing my face.

You can understand why he was so relaxed. *Miss Saigon* was, after all, a palpable hit, continuing to add to its pre-opening advance and generating standing ovations night after night. 'One great thing about the British subsidised theatre,' said Nick Hytner, three months after the opening, 'is that I can do three shows a year and you can't really tell which is a flop: I've had great notices for shows which people haven't been to see, and for operas which have had twenty-four performances in total over four years. The single most exciting thing for me about doing "Miss Saigon" is that, after eleven years in the theatre, for the first time I'm working for that wider public which is going to just get up and walk out if it's rubbish.'

But, even though they weren't walking out, the creative team still wasn't entirely satisfied. 'After the excitement of the opening night', said Schönberg, 'we knew there were still some problems with the beginning and the end of the show. And knowing that it's not running to perfection is motivation enough to get you back to work.' 'We can't wait to have another go,' declared Mackintosh.

To Bob Avian, there were one or two numbers (like 'Movie In My Mind') which could be improved; to Bill Brohn, some of the cameos in 'The Heat Is On In Saigon' needed sharpening up; and, as the weeks went by, Nick Hytner took to berating his own staging with a ferocity which excelled the show's worst reviews: 'I don't like "*Bui Doi*", I don't like the Bangkok number, I *hate* the hotel scene . . . ' Keeping a sense of proportion, Cameron Mackintosh thought it was a question of reining in the 'vein-slashing' – the tendency of a new musical on a big theme in a huge theatre to get a touch overheated. 'We want to calm it down, to let the power of the story and the music and lyrics breathe more. It's extraordinary, though, how if a show is basically right what in hindsight seems terribly important doesn't actually stop its motor.'

Nevertheless, in the spring of 1990, the producer and his team began planning extensive surgery on two key areas – the beginning and the end. 'We had to get away from the show,' said Mackintosh, 'and then go back to it. And, when we did, we realised that what we had actually done in the opening was bombard an audience who didn't yet know what world they were in. They got a feeling of it, but they didn't know where to look.'

John and the *bui doi* film

The first number in a musical has to be more than just the number that comes first. It has to define the show, both in terms of environment and style, bring the characters into focus and kick-start the story. As originally written, Kim was in danger of getting lost among the other bar girls in the beauty contest. In the rewrite, the Engineer tells us on whom we ought to be keeping an eye in the show's opening lines:

> Check it out! Look what I found!
> A new little country girl right off a truck.
> Tonight I spread the word we're doing 'Miss Saigon'.
> Fresh meat oughtta drag marines in – if we're in luck.
> (Gigi, get her a costume. Show off that young ass.)

The ending was perhaps in more obvious need of improvement. 'We haven't quite got it yet,' said Mackintosh. 'We don't allow the audience – or, indeed, ourselves – to get quite all the emotional juice out of the show. "The American Dream" is absolutely vital, but somewhere in that area we haven't got the show's tragic equilibrium back on the right scale. It's proving terribly difficult for us to fix.' But something had to be done about it. Steven

Spielberg and several others of the more analytical visitors to Drury Lane had identified it as the show's major weakness.

'Of course, it would have been more simple', says Schönberg, 'to go straight from the hotel scene with John, Chris and Ellen to Kim's suicide. But, in our first version, "The American Dream" was right for her situation: as the song was being sung, we saw her preparing her suicide. That's why at the end of the show, when she is ready to kill herself, "The American Dream" was supposed to come back, sung by a choir, like people enjoying it somewhere else while she is on the edge of the tragedy. It was a contour point of the action. But I don't know how much of that we achieved on stage. The song itself is proving to be so powerful that we are disturbing the drama, the story of Kim.'

It's one of the hardest traps to avoid: an individual number works so well that it throws the overall play off course. However, I don't think that was the problem here. Rather, the final scene seemed rushed, and the suicide not convincingly motivated. In the exotic *japoniste* atmosphere of earlier tellings of the story, such considerations didn't matter so much, and in any case, as Mackintosh puts it, 'Butterfly's ten minute warbling leaves you in no doubt what she's planning.' But, in a modern musical, the tone of Kim's final scene seemed at odds with what had gone before.

The authors began to consider their options. Clearly, Chris had to return, to see Kim one more time. But what sort of scene should it be? Should Kim try to seduce Chris? Or should she plead with him? 'There were so many options,' said Boublil, 'and then suddenly Richard put Claude-Michel and me back on our own track – back to that picture, the picture of a woman giving away her child.'

'What is the biggest emotional tragedy?' asked Maltby. 'The most brave, the most selfless act anyone can do? A mother giving away her child so that the child can have a life. That's what Claude-Michel and Alain saw in that photograph, and that's what we had to deliver in the scene. Kim wouldn't kill herself until she was sure of what would happen to Tam. The scene was in that photograph, the entire show was in that photo. Claude-Michel and Alain saw it, and that's what we had to get back to.' In June, the authors completed their new ending. 'At this point,' said Boublil at the end of a long day's rewrites, 'I have the impression that the show is at last finished.'

Not quite yet, as it transpired. The final scene required still more work. Schönberg went back to his piano and composed a heart-breaking melody, to which Boublil and Maltby set Kim's final thoughts. A week before *Miss Saigon*'s first anniversary, after Jonathan Pryce, Claire Moore and several others had already retired from the West End company, the new ending went in. Kim has

realised what must happen. She has to prepare her son for his new
life in America, a life she can never share:

> Now, big smile,
> One kiss, one more.
> Oh, my son, oh, my boy . . .
> Look at me one last time,
> Don't forget what you see . . .

In the new version, Kim's son goes off-stage before Kim kills
herself, her falling whole-tone motif and sardonic echoes of 'The
American Dream' play off against each other. With her son's future
secured, Kim shoots herself – as the last wandering line of the
translucent duet returns with cruel irony: 'How in one night have
we come . . . so far?'

At the same time as these changes to the book and score, the
physical production was also being rethought – principally for
New York's Broadway Theatre, where *Miss Saigon* was scheduled
to open in April 1991, but also for other venues. After all, Drury
Lane is a huge barn of a theatre. On Broadway, for example, it
would be difficult for the workers to raise Ho Chi Minh's statue;
it would have to be brought on ready made, so to speak. But this
technical adjustment was also merited dramatically: no scene in
the West End compared with the sight, eight times a week, of
paying Americans applauding the erection of a monument to Uncle
Ho. As happens too often in musicals, the form had outweighed
the content: a spectacular effect had distracted the audience from
the drama. Gradually, by working on the music, the staging and
finally the entrance of the statue itself, the *Saigon* team managed
in London to kill what had become deeply embarrassing applause.
They had no intention of making the same mistake in New York.

It was also decided to limit the number of 'trucks'. 'That's
because John and I,' said Hytner, 'are both confident that we can
now have that tight focus without bringing on little stages –
which is what "trucks" are.' In London, Kim's 'trucks' included
completely separate accommodation for her cubicle at Dreamland,
her hovel after the Vietcong's victory and her room at the club in
Bangkok – all of which took up too much space backstage. 'She's
a penniless Vietnamese girl,' sighed Mackintosh, 'and she's got
more property than Donald Trump.'

To the casual observer, these seemed merely routine preparations
for another British musical set to go around the globe. Mackintosh
wasn't so sure. 'First of all, I don't think of these shows as "British"
musicals. It just happens that there are two places in the world that
you can create musicals on a regular basis – one is London, the
other is New York – because that is where the majority of people

involved full-time in musicals live and work. All that has happened is that we are back in a European cycle. But I would be surprised if "Miss Saigon" went as many places as "Les Misérables". One reason is that Hugo wrote the greatest universal social novel of all time. Therefore, every country has a reason, beyond putting on the latest "hit musical", for doing "Les Misérables". The second is that "Miss Saigon" is an incredibly expensive production: it costs nearly three times as much as "Les Mis". And, third, "Miss Saigon" is a fiendishly difficult show to cast. The East/West interweaving is essential to the plot, the reason for the self-destruction and the tragedy. "Les Misérables", like "Fiddler on the Roof", is relatively actor-proof. I do not mean that in any way as an attack on the acting profession, but, as long as these shows are reasonably cast, the power of the story will still climax in a triumphant evening. "Miss Saigon", though, is actually too like "Madame Butterfly" for comfort: it requires performances from the principals of tremendous technical and emotional ability, just as you would expect to hear in an opera house. Unless you are thrilled by the vocal and acting performances of Kim and Chris, there is no heart to the show. The brilliant sardonic darkness of the piece is undoubtedly the Engineer, but despite his name he is not the engine of the show. They are.'

Furthermore, not only does Kim have to sing gloriously but she also has to be Oriental, which in many parts of the world where 'Les Mis' has played so successfully (Scandinavia, Central Europe) would demand a virtually impossible confluence of qualifications. On the demos for the orchestrations, Kim had been sung by Linzi Hateley, who played the title role in 'Carrie', the short-lived RSC horror musical (in every sense), and more recently had been stopping the show with 'On My Own' in 'Les Mis' in the West End. Throughout the casting sessions, Linzi's voice came back to haunt the creative team. 'We knew we'd never find an Asian girl who could do it like her,' says Mackintosh, 'but we realised that having a fantastic voice was just not enough.' The Engineer can be played by someone of any race – it's a fabulous one-off – but the love affair is symbolic of a wider cultural misunderstanding, and to try and do it with yellowface make-up would be faking it. For these various reasons, Mackintosh estimates that in the end there may be only a dozen or so productions of *Miss Saigon* as opposed to thirty or forty for 'Les Mis'.

He may be right. But, even so, that still makes it theatre on a scale never dreamt of by the sharpest operators in Broadway's golden age – men who never thought beyond Broadway, a road tour, and, if anybody in the West End or maybe a Commonwealth country was interested in doing it, they'd be happy to license it. In contrast, when I travelled by train through Germany and Austria recently, every platform of every station was advertising local productions of the same three Mackintosh musicals: *Cats*, 'Les Mis' and *Phantom*. Long before the people of Eastern Europe tore down the Iron Curtain, Mackintosh had smashed through it from the other side, sending his shows to Budapest, and to Gdynia in Poland. And, despite the number of overseas productions, travel agents around the world are still selling holiday packages built around the West End originals: five nights in London plus the chance to see *Cats* and *Phantom* or 'Les Mis' and *Miss Saigon*.

Whether or not the show's life beyond London is more limited than that of *Les Misérables, Miss Saigon* is still the major theatrical event of its day – as the producer himself underlined when he opened the New York box-office. The 1989–90 Broadway season had been hailed as the great rebirth of the American musical – on the strength, that is, of *City of Angels*, by two Broadway veterans, Larry Gelbart and Cy Coleman; a thirtieth anniversary revival of *Gypsy*; a stage version of the 1944 film *Meet Me in St Louis* by two writers in their late seventies; and a Broadway production of a Fifties out-of-town failure, *Grand Hotel*, by *three* writers in their late seventies.

At the 1990 Tony Awards, *City of Angels* and *Grand Hotel* obliterated Andrew Lloyd Webber's *Aspects of Love*. Both were amiable enough evenings in the theatre, but hardly blockbuster landmark hits. Even if their box-office receipts *had* gone through the roof, *Miss Saigon*'s were already climbing into the stratosphere, a difference of scale which Mackintosh emphasised by announcing a new top ticket price of $100 – $40 higher than his rivals.

Theatre is, in the end, made by individuals and not nation states, which is why so much of the British vs. American argument is ridiculous. In this case, though, there was a special poignancy. 'When "Miss Saigon" opens in New York,' said Richard Maltby, 'there's going to be a great sense of pain. This is the kind of show American musicals became great on, a popular entertainment on the major American event of contemporary history. *We* should have looked at ourselves in this way. There'll be a lot of sniffing on Broadway, but in the end a great sadness: this is the show *we* should have written.'

17 Calamity and Catharsis

The stage at the Royale Theatre, New York, where US auditions were held

John Napier began redesigning the set for the Broadway Theatre production in May 1990. A month later, a campaign against the proposed Broadway production of *Miss Saigon* began, initiated and fuelled by a small group of American Equity members. This was to lead to one of the most serious crises in contemporary American theatre; a modern-day Dreyfus Case that would split the artistic community, ignite a huge controversy and become the focus of editorial comment in almost every American newspaper.

The issue was Jonathan Pryce, whose London triumph in the role of the Engineer in *Miss Saigon* had earned him both the Olivier Award and universal critical acclaim. From Pryce's glorious opening night in London, there had been little doubt in Cameron Mackintosh's mind that, should Pryce want to open the Broadway production in that role, the part was his and no one else's. Pryce *was* eager to do it, and so from the start of the planning for the Broadway production, due to open on 11 April 1991, the entire production team assumed that the role had been cast.

A hard core of Asian members of the American Equity Association (AEA), however, determined that Pryce should not have the part, and they almost succeeded. In the process, Cameron Mackintosh was forced to cancel the Broadway production of *Miss Saigon*. The crisis was to become *the* conversational topic not only in New York, but wherever theatrical matters were of concern, whether in London, Paris, Milan, Tokyo, Berlin or Manila. The issues raised were important, involving on the one hand the rights and prerogatives of the *Miss Saigon* creative production team, and on the other the determination of ethnic minorities to protect and advance their cause. Though the broader issues remained unresolved and continued to be hotly debated long after the *Miss Saigon* affair was settled, the drama played out in the summer of 1990 did have the merit of drawing attention to the grievances voiced by a minority of American Asian members of AEA, using *Miss Saigon* as a lightning-rod issue.

Shortly after the London opening, Mackintosh took Alan Eisenberg, the Executive Secretary of AEA into his confidence, and told him that because of Jonathan Pryce's huge success as the Engineer, he was the obvious choice to open in the part in New York. At the same time, however, Mackintosh was not sure that Pryce, who had never before done such a long stint in a single role, would want to open in New York for a further nine-month commitment. He would only know for certain by April 1990, once Pryce was half-way through his London engagement. When this time came, Pryce confirmed that he wanted to open in New York, and at the end of May 1990 Eisenberg unofficially told Mackintosh and Bernard Jacobs, head of the Shubert Organisation, that he could see no problem at all in Pryce's doing so – approval, he added, would be a mere formality.

Pryce as the Engineer had brought the house down in London. The quality of the performance of this Eurasian pimp figure – part-narrator, part-witness – was crucial to the success of any *Miss Saigon* production. Kim was, of course, its star, but to some extent the Engineer's role was comparable to that of the Emcee in *Cabaret*, who literally 'drove' the show. In rehearsal, Pryce had been more than a performer; he, along with Hytner, had elaborated on and to some extent 'invented' some of the intricacies of his part. Mackintosh knew that a British-born piece of musical theatre, written and composed by two Frenchmen, would come under intense American scrutiny, and that he needed the strongest possible cast for the strongest possible impact. *Miss Saigon*'s creative production team knew that Pryce's performance would be a determining element in the Broadway show's artistic success.

American Equity, like its British counterpart, exists to defend the interests and livelihoods of its members, and all foreigners have to be approved by AEA before they can work in the American theatre. In the case of Jonathan Pryce, however, AEA's approval should have been purely technical, for according to American Equity rules, recognised stars are automatically granted permission to perform in the United States. Jonathan Pryce *was* a star, and not only as a result of his award-winning Engineer performance: some years before, he had received a Tony Award for his performance in Trevor Griffiths's *Comedians*; in 1984 he played the leading role in *Accidental Death of An Anarchist*, and since then his reputation had been boosted by his roles in two critically acclaimed films – *Brazil* and *1984*.

In June 1990, Mackintosh took a vacation, blissfully unaware that Pryce's acceptance of the role in New York was set to become a highly controversial issue. The crisis came, completely by surprise, in a fanfare of publicity, in the second week of July 1990 – less than two months before final casting decisions were due to be made.

It all began with a petition from New York's 'Pan Asian Repertory Theatre' signed by its artistic director, Tisa Chang. In a letter to Alan Eisenberg dated 6 June, she wrote expressing 'our dissatisfaction with the AEA' for allowing the role of the Engineer to go to a 'non-Asian foreign actor, Jonathan Pryce'.

Ms Chang, who clearly could not have seen Pryce's London

performance, wrote that 'The insensitivity of this action could only be compared to having the role of Boy Willie in *The Piano Lesson* portrayed by a man in blackface. It is a shame that Cameron Mackintosh and the AEA both believe that painting a Caucasian actor yellow is an acceptable action.' While commending Mackintosh's prowess as a commercial producer, she added that 'Mr Pryce's performance in *Miss Saigon* was not prominently mentioned prior to his Olivier Award . . . With this action', she concluded, 'Equity is sending the following message to its minority members: we will support your right to work as long as your role is not central to the play.'

Twelve days later, another letter, this time addressed to Colleen Dewhurst, President of American Equity, showed that the campaign was gathering strength, was carefully orchestrated and had some powerful backers. B.D. Wong, the Chinese-American star of *M. Butterfly*, wrote seeking her support 'on an issue of racism' to protest 'a practice which I thought was dying'.

He continued: 'It is time for me and the Asian American community to stand in the way of yellowface. I strongly believe that the granting of a 'visa' [to Jonathan Pryce] would send a dangerous and detrimental racial message to Cameron Mackintosh, to British Equity, to the membership of our own AEA, and perhaps most frighteningly to the ticket-buying public at large which would view such an abomination of casting naïvely.

'The time for actors of color to be playing "their own" roles is certainly *now*. We cannot even begin to fight for *non-traditional* casting if audiences are not given permission to accept us enacting characters of our *own* colors . . . Allowing such a blatant example of high profile, racially false casting in our own back yard because British Equity has not taken care of its own members the way AEA aims to would be passive and self-destructive.'

B.D. Wong also canvassed Asian Equity members to join in his protest, enclosing a suggested 'form letter' for them to sign. This, dated 21 June, read:

'I am writing to demand protection of my rights as an Equity actor of color by calling for rejection of producer Cameron Mackintosh's application which would allow a non-Asian British actor to play a leading, specifically Asian role in the forthcoming American production of *Miss Saigon*.

'There is no doubt in my mind of the irreparable damage to my rights as an actor that would be wrought if (at the threshold of the 21st century) Asian actors are kept from bringing their unique dignity to the specifically Asian roles in *Miss Saigon* . . . At this time in history, blackface is wrong, yellowface is wrong. Only Equity and her Alien Committee has the power to stop this ridiculous notion, or else it will magnify and multiply itself so fast that it will become an *hourly* issue which Equity simply is not equipped to fight . . . Force Cameron Mackintosh and future producers to cast their productions with racial authenticity.'

In an accompanying note, urging fellow-actors to sign, Wong was even more explicit, his racial appeal unequivocal: 'We may *never* be able to do the *real* work we dream to do if a Caucasian actor with taped eyelids hops on the Concorde . . . Chances to nail the big guys like this don't come often. Let's do it.' In an interview, one of the leaders of the anti-Pryce AEA lobby claimed that as the Engineer, Jonathan Pryce came on stage at the Theatre Royal 'painted yellow' with 'taped slit eyes, fake bushy eyebrows and a wig'. The truth was that, in London, Pryce *had* used prosthetics on the eyes, and this had never been an issue with Equity in London, or with its Asian community. As soon as the campaign against him began in America, he stopped using them. He had never worn a wig nor tampered with his eyebrows, and had not even used theatrical make-up – just a Clinique bronzing lotion.

The implicit threat to his producer's prerogative (for according to AEA rules, Mackintosh knew, his choice of Pryce was unassailable) was bad enough. What was even more shocking to him was the violently hostile tone of some of the statements made by American Asian members of AEA. In London, the creative production team's relations with the Asians in the cast were marked by friendship and trust. Suddenly, in the United States, they had become the enemy. Mackintosh didn't know what he resented most: the language of the petition to AEA debasing *Miss Saigon* to the level of a 'minstrel show' or the implication that he himself harboured racist sentiments. The unexpected campaign against him, with its overtly aggressive, resentful overtones, threatened to make proper casting and rehearsal almost impossible. By introducing the notion of racial privilege under the guise of multi-racial equality, pitting Asian actor against Asian actor, it threatened the whole climate of pre-production and rehearsal time. It implied that candidates at auditions would claim legitimate priority on the ground of race alone, with possible pickets, media attention and open confrontation during rehearsals, subjecting Jonathan Pryce and Nicholas Hytner to intolerable strain.

Mackintosh was well aware of the need for a dedicated, united production team in the weeks leading up to such an important première. He had witnessed enough failures resulting from off-stage conflict to know that harmonious collaboration was a key to success on Broadway. No production could possibly get under way with a vocal, hostile caucus of Equity members threatening to sabotage it, trying to impose their own choice of actors using race as sole criterion. The anti-Pryce campaigners seemed not to know or perhaps did not care that while seeking performers for the original London production, Mackintosh had already cast his net unprecedentedly wide in the USA, auditioning hundreds of male and female Asian-Americans singers in New York, San Francisco, Los Angeles and Hawaii. Johnson-Liff Casting Associates, the firm involved in *Miss Saigon* from the start, had conducted what was far and away the most exhaustive search ever made for Asian talent, compiling a list of over a thousand names. And as Tommy Aguilar, the artistic director of the American Theatre Company in Hawaii, pointed out in a letter to AEA executives, the *Miss Saigon* creative production team had, for the original London production of *Miss Saigon*, been the only one ever to prospect for talent in Hawaii. 'For the first time ever,' he wrote, 'actors in Hawaii actually felt that someone cared about their talent and that they might have a chance to really work in the professional theatre.'

As well as the anti-Pryce lobbyists, American Equity executives appeared not to be aware of the in-depth search for the *Miss Saigon* cast, or at least dismissed these efforts as irrelevant. To the general public, Mackintosh and his creative production team were portrayed as a bunch of unscrupulous, exclusively business-orientated tycoons, deliberately spurning America's Asian community.

Petitions, mostly from black and Asian Equity members, flooded AEA headquarters in July, but the majority of AEA members had no idea of the extent of the campaign. And Mackintosh himself, though privately aware that he now faced a major crisis, deliberately refrained from aggravating it by launching a counter-offensive at this stage, hoping that the AEA Executives would be able to contain it, and comply with their contractual obligations. Mackintosh submitted a formal application to AEA on behalf of Jonathan Pryce on 20 July. During lunch with Cameron Mackintosh on 21 July, Colleen Dewhurst remarked that it made little difference who played the Engineer 'since 25 million dollars-worth of tickets have already been sold'. This, perhaps, more than anything else, dismayed and infuriated Mackintosh, for it dismissed as irrelevant the standards he had always struggled to impose. On 24 July, bowing to the activists but postponing its formal decision, the American Equity Association, announced that the casting of Jonathan Pryce would be 'especially insensitive and an affront to the Asian community'.

In a letter to Bernard Jacobs, whose Broadway Theatre was to house *Miss Saigon*, Mackintosh wrote:

'This issue is not only about Jonathan Pryce but also about the future occupants of the role of the Engineer. [The AEA statement] is tantamount to its morally barring the bulk, if not the entire, potential source of leading contenders for this role – American

Equity's major Caucasian actors. The sort of inquiries so far received by us asking consideration for the role of the Engineer have been from agents of actors of the stature of Joel Grey and Christopher Lloyd.'

Mackintosh said he was astonished that the AEA Council had made a public statement without consulting its members by referendum. 'The colour of one's skin cannot be the only criterion for casting. Talent has to be the primary consideration.'

'In all my other productions', he wrote, 'we have very willingly had to spread our casting net as wide as possible to find actors of the right calibre. As a character, the Engineer is the archetypal outsider who excludes himself from every community and we therefore feel that the part can be played by actors of any race.'

However, on 7 August, AEA formally turned down Mackintosh's request to have Jonathan Pryce perform the role of the Engineer. In a statement afterwards, it said that 'after a long and emotional debate' it could not 'appear to condone the casting of a Caucasian actor in the role of a Eurasian'. This, it went on, 'is an affront to the Asian community'. In a curious attempt to blame Mackintosh himself, the Equity statement added that 'the producer retains the right to bring this matter to arbitration. Should Mr Mackintosh refuse to avail himself of this contractually prescribed remedy and cancel or postpone his production of *Miss Saigon*, lost employment and lost revenues are ultimately his responsibility.' In a final sting, it said it was trying to 'schedule a meeting to review the casting practices of not only *Les Misérables* but other plays in which the lack of ethnic actors is dramatically evident,' inviting the media to 'take an in-depth look at ethnic casting in the American theater instead of sensationalizing one example.'

Both Mackintosh and AEA knew that had he gone for arbitration he would win. But this was out of the question, for it would only have exacerbated existing tensions, and allowed AEA 'activists' to continue their activity, while allowing their AEA colleagues to audition for parts.

The question was one of principle, over which Mackintosh was not prepared to compromise. Many of the Equity Executive Council members, unacquainted with Cameron Mackintosh personally, remained convinced that with a record sum in pre-sold tickets he would eventually be forced to back down, and find a way to salvage the $25-million advance, even if this meant sacrificing Jonathan Pryce. Mackintosh's colleagues and friends, however, knew him better, and were sure that this was something he would never do. By this time, he was in any case slightly weary of the battle into which he had been dragged, conscious that he was being used as a target by a group of lobbyists eager to score points in a quintessentially American artistic controversy that went far beyond

Miss Saigon. He was not alone in feeling that one of the covert reasons for the crisis was resentment that British musicals had come to dominate the Broadway stage. He also detested the image of him that was being projected: that of a high-handed mogul, devoid of sensitivity and scornful of the aspirations of ethnic minorities – an image so greatly at odds with reality, as his friends and theatrical colleagues knew, as to be laughable. Particularly galling was the fact that, for all the publicity the affair generated, and the accusations being bandied about, none of the Equity Executives who had ruled against him had actually taken the trouble to see *Miss Saigon* in London – not even Alan Eisenberg, whom Cameron Mackintosh had invited to the show's première.

Thus, on 8 August 1990 Mackintosh took out an ad in the *New York Times.* Headed MISS SAIGON CANCELLED, it announced that there was to be no Broadway production. It added that the creative team of *Miss Saigon* found the AEA decision 'a disturbing violation of the principles of artistic integrity and freedom'.

In a simultaneous statement to the press, Mackintosh said the debate was not only about casting, 'but the art of acting itself': 'We passionately disapprove of stereotype casting, which is why we continue to champion freedom of artistic choice. Racial barriers can only undermine the very foundations of our profession.' Jonathan Pryce had been rejected 'solely on the grounds that he is a Caucasian . . . The inaccurate and inflammatory statements which Equity has made concerning *Miss Saigon* have served only to create a poisonous atmosphere in which creativity and artistic freedom cannot function or survive . . . Racial prejudice does seem to have triumphed over creative freedom. A sad statement on the current state of the arts in America.

'It is particularly sad and ironic that this controversy should surround a piece of theatre such as *Miss Saigon,* a tragic love story in which a young woman sacrifices her life to ensure that her Amerasian son may find a better life in America. Actors' Equity, cloaking itself behind a veil of self-righteous hypocrisy, has now gained its own sacrifice, and it is called *Miss Saigon.*' Privately, Mackintosh felt relieved that the crisis was over at last, but sad that the circumstances forced him to ask himself whether he would ever want to present any new shows on Broadway.

Neither Mackintosh, nor American Equity, can have anticipated the storm that followed, or the extent of editorial comment in US newspapers, almost all of it in support of Mackintosh. Nor was discussion confined to New York. In London, Peter Plouviez, the General Secretary of British Equity, condemned the AEA decision, pointing out that had Pryce been American, AEA would not have been able to stop him being cast. 'This offends us,' he said.

'When is censorship not censorship? When it's being exercised by Actors' Equity,' wrote former New York mayor, Ed Koch in the *New York Post*. After seeing *Miss Saigon* in London, Frank Rich wrote in the *New York Times* that Pryce's performance 'is as essential to *Miss Saigon* as Mr Grey's was to *Cabaret . . .* Equity could hardly have picked a worse example to argue the case than the Engineer in *Miss Saigon*.' Colleen Dewhurst's description of *Miss Saigon* as a 'minstrel show' was, he wrote, 'demagogically misrepresenting the role and Mr Pryce's performance. Or, worse, is it possible that she has not even bothered to see the fellow actor whose work she has branded as perpetuating a racial stereotype?' By barring Pryce 'under the disingenuous guise of promoting democratic principles,' Actors' Equity, said Rich, 'has, I fear, stumbled into its very own Vietnam'.

Prominent American Equity members, including Charlton Heston and John Malkovich, threatened to quit if the ban on Pryce was not reversed. Soon, AEA offices all over the US were deluged with letters, petitions and phone calls from members, all asking for another hearing.

The uproar was such that the AEA Council, at a special meeting held at AEA members' request, reversed its decision a week later, in the same week that Jonathan Pryce ended his Drury Lane run. After noting that Pryce indeed 'qualified as a star', and that the Union 'had applied an honest and moral principle in an inappropriate manner,' Equity's communiqué went on to repeat at length the arguments justifying its original stand, but ended with the following words: 'Actors' Equity welcomes Jonathan Pryce and wishes Cameron Mackintosh's production of *Miss Saigon* a long and prosperous run.'

For Cameron Mackintosh and his team, however, the statement was not good enough. It acknowledged that its veto of Jonathan Pryce had been not so much a mistake as an 'unconstitutional' decision in the light of its own statutes. But its heavy emphasis on the issues that had brought about the crisis in the first place boded ill for the future. He knew there was nothing AEA could do to stop individual members from demonstrating their hostility to Jonathan Pryce, but what he needed was a formal pledge that AEA would not throw its weight behind them, as it had at the start of the crisis.

Mackintosh delayed replying for several days. When he did react, he made it clear that he was unprepared to reinstate the production without Equity's guarantee that the atmosphere would change, and that its members would not continue their campaign in other, more subtle ways. What was needed, he said, was a formal understanding between him and Equity that casting and pre-production would take place without intimidation, recriminations, innuendos or indirect pressures on Equity members.

Alain Boublil, Vincent Liff
and Cameron Mackintosh
at US casting session

Responding formally to the Equity statement, on behalf of *Miss Saigon's* creative production team, Mackintosh said he was 'enormously grateful for the overwhelming support for our position from the membership of Equity, the theatrical profession, the public and the press,' but that 'I cannot in good conscience reschedule the production in the absence of a positive working environment, and an understanding, agreed to without reservation at all, that artistic freedom of choice cannot be compromised, and that our efforts to cast *Miss Saigon* with the best available talent will be supported . . . I also believe that it is essential that we forge a constructive working relationship with Actors' Equity and the Asian community for *Miss Saigon* to proceed.'

An interesting aspect of the *Miss Saigon* protest was that the minority group raising the ethnicity issue was not black but Asian. What provoked the crisis was an awareness that the *New York Times*, in an important editorial, referred to as 'a new tribalism, a heightened awareness of ethnic and racial separateness'. The new trend, it said, was 'in a proliferation of small cultures – an ethnic culture, a racial culture, a woman's, a gay's, a black's culture. Everybody seems to be looking at the world through the brightly coloured lens of his or her own particular group.' This, in turn, threatened to usher in a new era of conformity and sanctimoniousness.

Cameron Mackintosh recognised that the controversy had had the merit of 'focusing public attention upon the many injustices, both past and present, which have been endured by Asians and other artists of colour in the American theatre. This is long overdue.' What was now required, he said, was 'a firm commitment from Equity to work with us sensibly and practically on all casting problems, to ensure that *Miss Saigon* is able to be performed to the highest possible standard wherever and for however long it plays in the United States.' In his statement before the final Equity talks began, Mackintosh thanked them 'for making us aware of all the past and present discrimination and injustice that the Asian acting community and all actors of colour have suffered and continue to suffer. I absolutely accept that they have acted sincerely and passionately to bring this issue to light.'

Meetings with Equity got under way, quietly at first, but with a constant undercurrent of tension that developed into rows on several occasions. Both sides agreed that the talks should be conducted in private, and that there should be no further press 'leaks' which might exacerbate matters and cause the 'activists' in AEA to renew their campaign.

Had the original AEA ruling barring Pryce been sustained, many producers and directors might have been deterred from staging productions and risking the kind of crisis faced by Cameron

Mackintosh and his production team in the summer of 1990. Mackintosh was strong enough to challenge the decision because his career as a producer would not have been seriously affected by the cancellation of the show: the loss of the pre-sale advance, amounting to $25 million, was something he was fully prepared to accept. In the eyes of many leading US producers and directors, Cameron Mackintosh's firm, principled stand saved the American theatre from a potentially damaging predicament; several told him in private that they themselves would not have had the nerve to act as he had.

A formal agreement between AEA and the *Miss Saigon* creative production team was finally approved by both sides, and on 6 October 1990, auditioning for the Broadway production of *Miss Saigon* began without any media fanfare. The following day, an ad in the *New York Times* announced: THE HEAT IS BACK ON! and advance sales of tickets resumed. Ironically, the publicity resulting from the *Miss Saigon* crisis caused a number of Asian performers who might not otherwise have heard of the play, to contact the production team.

It soon became apparent, as the auditioning process unfolded, that a successful *Miss Saigon* run in America would stretch Amerasian talent resources to the limit. Though American Equity has 40,000 members, only a tiny proportion – some 400 – is of Asian heritage. People came to audition from as far away as Anchorage, Alaska and Honolulu. The staff at Johnson–Liff Casting Associates had by this time compiled an exhaustive inventory of Amerasian singing and dancing talent. They were, however, well aware that should *Miss Saigon* generate companies in Los Angeles, San Francisco or Chicago (as *Les Misérables* had done) they would be hard pressed to provide sufficient performers. Ironically, therefore, the greatest threat to the future of *Miss Saigon* in the USA was not the virulence of a minority of Amerasian Equity activists, but the small size of the Amerasian acting and dancing community in relation to the needs of the *Miss Saigon* production team.

Though experts readily acknowledge the extraordinary proliferation of musical talent in the Philippines, few can explain it. Early exposure to Western culture, the importance of the Catholic Church (including its singing liturgy), the Spanish cultural heritage and the extraordinary popularity of American jazz, pop music and blues are all contributing factors. Throughout the Philippines, there are strong theatrical traditions, and even in remote country areas the calibre of performers is likely to be far higher than in equivalent areas in Europe or even in the United States. All over Asia, with the exception of China, Vietnam and North Korea, where foreign performers are – with a few notable exceptions – unwelcome, night-clubs, dance-halls, jazz groups and piano-bars

Above and *overleaf* Auditioning for parts in *Miss Saigon* on Broadway

are likely to feature Filipino talent, and musicians and dancers are one of the Philippines' largely unrecognised but essential 'invisible exports'.

At the New York auditions, one of the few candidates to be cast on the spot (for the role of Thuy) was Barry Bernal, a twenty-seven-year-old American of Filipino descent. Of the eight 'finalists' for the starring role of Kim, six were of Filipino origin – including three well known singers who had flown from Manila to New York to compete for the part. Among them, too, were candidates for the role of Gigi, one of whom, the well known Filipino singing star Dulce, so entranced the production team that they gave her, as they had Pryce, a rare ovation.

The final auditions for *Miss Saigon* in New York were exciting because they showed the Broadway production was likely to have a new dimension, that it would be even more electrifying visually than the original London production. One of the great assets of Broadway lay in the number of those auditioning for parts who displayed dancing as well as acting and singing skills. From the very first few minutes of a dance routine run-through for potential candidates, it was clear that the 'American Dream' sequence would be a sensation on the American stage.

Even after casting began, an undercurrent of hostile resentment prevailed in among some of the original lobby's leaders, especially on the West Coast. In statements, speeches and newspaper interviews, they continued to deplore what they regarded as American Equity's 'climbdown', and there were even rumours of a breakaway group setting up its own, radical union.

It would be wrong to dismiss the protests of AEA minority groups, both Asian and black, as simply malicious or narrowminded. Both David Henry Hwang, author of the prize-winning play, *M. Butterfly*, and its star, B.D. Wong, spoke eloquently and movingly about the frustrations, concealed for so long in American society, that black and Asian actors had endured; and the celebrated producer Joe Papp noted that Asian actors 'have been treated as caricatures for hundreds of years, and now they have had an opportunity to take a very powerful position on racism'. That these issues were coming to the fore was part and parcel of the change underlying American society in the Nineties.

The irony of the situation was not lost on the production team: there would have been no *Miss Saigon* without the Vietnam War and its many social and psychological repercussions. Now, in turn, *Miss Saigon* itself had become an issue in America, the controversy surrounding it provoking a dramatic confrontation in a country which had been profoundly altered by the fall of Saigon. To the bewilderment of its creators, what had begun as a show had

190

become a landmark in the multi-racial history of a changing, post-Vietnam America. The experience gave special significance to the haunting cry that is both a recurring melody in *Miss Saigon*, and is its final, heart-breaking lament and unanswerable question: 'How in one night have we come . . . so far?'

Index